Value Creation within the Construction Industry

Corporate Finance and Governance

Herausgegeben von Dirk Schiereck

Band 3

PETER LANG

Frankfurt am Main · Berlin · Bern · Bruxelles · New York · Oxford · Wien

Joachim Vogt

Value Creation within the Construction Industry

A Study of Strategic Takeovers

PETER LANG
Internatior aler Verlag der Wissenschaften

Bibliographic Information published by the Deutsche Nationalbibliothek
The Deutsche Nationalbibliothek lists this publication in the Deutsche Nationalbibliografie; detailed bibliographic data is available in the internet at http://dnb.d-nb.de.

Zugl.: European Business School, Univ., Diss., 2009

Cover Design:
Olaf Glöckler, Atelier Platen, Friedberg

D 1540
ISSN 1869-537X
ISBN 978-3-631-60251-5

www.peterlang.de

Preface

Writing a PhD thesis is an incredible challenge. I could not have completed this demanding project without the selfless contribution of numerous supporters. To these individuals, family, friends, and colleagues, I dedicate this work.

I would like to begin by thanking my first supervisor Prof. Dr. Dirk Schiereck. His professional advice, constructive input and challenging questions were essential to me in writing the dissertation. He also supported me however he was able. I hold him in high esteem and offer my highest gratitude in exchange for his support. In addition I am grateful for the valuable professional input of my second supervisor, Prof. Dr. Nico Rottke. I am particularly grateful for his efforts and advice during preparations for my final examination.

Recognizing my professional peers, I reflect upon the inspiring time spent with my colleagues at the Department Finance, Accounting and Real Estate. I would especially like to thank Dr. Mark Mietzner and Felix Miebs for sharing their impressive knowledge in corporate finance and programming. In addition to the crucial intellectual contribution they made to my thesis, they also count amongst my good friends.

I am grateful to my close American friends, Katherine Abbott and Mark Lewis, who offered me continuous motivation to excel. They also donated their time and patience in proofreading my dissertation in its successive incarnations. I thank them for improving the elementary quality of the thesis.

Without best friends, I would not have completed this challenging journey. Matthäus Sielecki supported me unconditionally, in every task and at every time. Matthäus' strong encouragement and altruistic character enabled me to succeed in every challenge, including writing this dissertation. Benjamin Reinbold is a life-long friend on whom I can always rely, regardless of the situation or task. Patrick Heinecke and Georg Merholz showed up for me when I needed good, capable friends.

I devote a significant part of this dissertation to my family. My mother, father and siblings have always been there, making every effort to help me realize my happiness. They provide me with the inner strength to cope with life's challenges, including my doctoral studies and more.

Finally, I offer the most important dedication, to my beloved partner Melanie Redetzki who took this journey with me. She patiently witnessed my every thought and feeling, my every doubt and fear. She also served as a capable peer, helping me formulate my ideas. Her love and empathy were the essential elements in discovering my voice and finding my right path. Naturally, my most profound gratitude belongs to her.

Joachim Vogt

Foreword

Which motives initiate managers to merge or to acquire other corporations? While there is a long-lasting history of academic research on M&A in a cross-industry context, our knowledge about industry specific drivers of M&A is more than limited. Given this background, the construction industry is an attractive segment to address questions on M&A motives – as it is on the one hand a very fragmented industry and on the other hand a very internationally oriented segment which is traditionally organized by cross-company production structures. Construction companies are very familiar in integrating outside knowledge and competencies into internal teams resulting in partnering solutions which are needed to realize very challenging construction project.

In his thesis, Mr. Vogt makes an effort to answer the question why firms in the construction industry follow M&A strategies and how successful they are in their transactions. This is not only a remarkable endeavor because Mr. Vogt uses some hand selected unique datasets, but in particular, because he presents state-of-the-art analyses which are competitive and meet highest international standards.

The thesis on hand carefully identifies and addresses open research questions related to M&A strategies and M&A performance in a very specific industry. Its primary objective was to identify short-term and long-run drivers of the M&A success for different types of M&A transactions in various sub-segments of the construction industry by analyzing stock price and accounting data. Thusly objectifying managerial action allows deriving recommendations for financing practice. Another focus of the thesis concerns the use of case study methodology to analyze the consequences resulting from the critical selection of acquisition targets in a still hardly consolidated industry segment that only generates overall operational growth beyond the German home market of the transaction partners under consideration. The documented empirical evidence provides significant negative value added for the involved parties. Defensive acquisitions in stagnating regional markets seem to destroy shareholder value.

Mr. Vogt fully achieves the objectives of this dissertation. The analysis contains many intriguing and surprising results which make this thesis an interesting read I highly recommend to corporate finance researchers and practitioners. I wish for a high, due circulation of this dissertation.

Prof. Dr. Dirk Schiereck

Table of Contents

List of Tables

List of Figures

List of Abbreviations

ACS	Actividades de Construccion y Servicios
AG	Aktiengesellschaft
BHAR	Buy-and-Hold Abnormal Return
CAR	Cumulated Abnormal Return
CAAR	Cumulated Average Abnormal Return
CB	Combined Portfolio
CDAX	Composite Deutscher Aktienindex
CEO	Chief Executive Officer
DSI	Dyckerhoff Systems International
DYWIDAG	Dyckerhoff und Widmann AG
E	España
EBIT	Earnings before Interest and Taxes
EBT	Earnings before Taxes
EPS	Earnings per Share
GDP	Gross Domestic Product
GmbH	Gesellschaft mit beschränkter Haftung
ICE	Intercity Express
IPO	Initial Public Offering
IRL	Ireland
ISIC	International Standards of Industrial Classification
M&A	Mergers and Acquisitions
M/B	Market to Book
MV	Market Value
MTBV	Market to Book Value
n.a.	not available
NObs	Number of Observations
OLS	Ordinary Least Square

PLC	Public Limited Company
PPP	Public Private Partnership
RBS	Royal Bank of Scotland
R&D	Research and Development
REIT	Real Estate Investment Trust
ROCE	Return on Capital Employed
ROE	Return on Equity
SIC	Standard Industrial Classification
UBW	Universal-Bau Walter
UK	United Kingdom
US	United States
USD	United States Dollar
WTB	Walter-Thosti-Boswau

List of Symbols

$\overline{\alpha}_i$	Market model based Alpha (y-axis intercept) of firm *i*
$\overline{\alpha}_w$	Market model based Alpha (y-axis intercept) for Walter Bau
$AR_{i,t}$	Abnormal return for firm *i* over time interval *t*
$AR_{w,t}$	Abnormal return of Walter Bau over time interval *t*
$\overline{\beta}_i$	Market model based Beta for firm *i*
$\overline{\beta}_w$	Market model based Beta for Walter Bau
$BHAR_{i,[t,T]}$	Buy-and-hold abnormal return of firm *i* from point in time *t* until *T*
$BHAR_{j,[t,T]}$	Buy-and-hold abnormal return of the reference portfolio *j* from point in time *t* until *T*
$BHAR_{w,[t,T]}$	Buy-and-hold abnormal return of Walter Bau from point in time *t* until *T*
$CAR_{c,[t,T]}$	Cumulated abnormal return for the combined entity *c* from point in time *t* until *T*
$CAR_{i,[t,T]}$	Cumulated abnormal return for firm *i* from point in time *t* until *T*
$CAR_{w,[t,T]}$	Cumulated abnormal return for Walter Bau from point in time *t* until *T*
$CAAR_{i,[t,T]}$	Cumulated average abnormal return for firm *i* from point in time *t* until *T*
$i=1,\ldots,N$	Index of observations of sample firms
$j=1,\ldots,N$	Index of observations of reference portfolios
MV_i	Market Value of the target *i* one day before the event window
MV_w	Market Value of Walter Bau one day before the event window
n_b	Sample extraction of the original Sample Size N
$R_{i,t}$	Stock Return of firm *i* over time interval *t*

$\overline{R}_{i,t}$	Market Model based expected Stock Return of firm i over time ^ interval t
$\overline{R}_{m,t}$	Return of Market Index m over time interval t
$R_{w,t}$	Stock Return of Walter Bau over interval t
$\overline{R}_{w,t}$	Market Model based expected Stock Return of Walter Bau over time interval t
$t = 1,\ldots, T$	Index of time

1 Introduction

1.1 Research Overview and Objectives

Mergers & Acquisitions (M&A) and the construction industry have one thing in common. They both build new and unique entities. Due to their uniqueness the created entities differ in size, complexity and their character. Construction entities are unique as e.g. an office can be 100 or 1000 feet high at varying footprints, design, material inputs or other parameters inducing different challenges on the architecture of the building. Some of the ways in which M&A are unique is the strategy that is required, the companies who bid, the culture the involved parties comprise and the location they encompass. Companies have several challenges to address when considering M&A transactions: Is a horizontal acquisition of competitors enhancing the market power and entailing synergies for the merging parties or are the employees reluctant to cooperate in the new entity causing extraordinary expenses instead of synergies? Can the vertical integration of suppliers raise the efficiency of the production process or is the consequent dependency on the integrated supplier detrimental? Does lateral diversification lead to substantial benefits, as revenue streams are distributed and the independency from the core business is increased or causes this M&A type crucial difficulties due to the insufficient knowledge of the acquired business? Furthermore, the geographical focus of the M&A transaction significantly influences the acquisition decision. Should international diversification be preferred to national consolidation in the course of the globalizing world economy or is the familiarity with the national culture more important for a successful integration? In addition, the financial static of the acquisition is of major relevance for the success of the transaction. The acquisition requires an adequate funding and a stable financial foundation for operating and competing successfully. Consequently, the M&A success depends on the shape of the static as well as the design of the architecture of the new entity.

Several studies have already investigated the wealth effects of mergers and acquisitions in cross-industrial surveys. Overall, most studies document negative or no wealth impacts for the acquirer and positive effects for the targets indicating that wealth is transferred from the acquirer shareholders to the target shareholders (Loughran and Vijh, 1997; Andrade et al., 2001; Bruner, 2002; Jovanovic and Barguinsky, 2004; Moeller et al., 2005). Nevertheless, the studies often report heterogeneous results with a high variance of the abnormal returns, as industry specific wealth effects remain unconsidered (Gregory and McCorriston, 2005). However, when observing the M&A in one industry, these general effects may shift, as every industry has its own peculiarities.

This applies particularly to the construction industry. The worldwide construction industry is characterized by high fragmentation and in several countries faces supply overcapacities of construction services (Euroconstruct, 2007; Engineering News Record, 2006). This often causes price competition deterioration among the construction firms for new projects. The construction firms calculate the costs as low as possible for the construction projects neglecting any unforeseen incidents on the construction site. In addition, as each construction project is unique and has to be newly designed, planned and conducted, an exact predictability of the costs and profits is difficult to achieve. This situation creates shrinking profits or even a loss of the project as most incidents occur during the construction process (Glawon, 2009). Finally, the size of a construction firm often determines whether the company is perceived by the customer as capable to handle big-scale construction projects. For example, for big-scale civil engineering projects, a construction firm requires capital intensive machinery. This machinery can usually only be afforded by big construction firms. Since however, civil-engineering projects and other big-scale projects are mostly more lucrative than smaller construction operations, it becomes attractive for construction firms to reach that critical size, which enables them to operate such projects (Delaney and Wamuziri, 2004).

To overcome these burdens many construction firms have used M&A as a remedy. Some construction firms intend to reduce the capacities on the market by purchasing a market competitor thereby trying to increase the market power as well as their profitability. Other firms diversify their business into related and also unrelated businesses of the construction sector in order to spread their revenue sources. Due to the accelerating globalization, several customers demand international construction services. Hence, construction firms often expand their business to other countries by acquiring a foreign construction firm. Furthermore, as construction volumes on several markets as Japan or Germany dropped severely in the period from 1995–2004, intensifying the competition for new contracts, many construction firms in these markets extended their business to construction markets with growing volumes (Rice, 2007; Statistisches Bundesamt, 2008; Ministry of Land, Infrastructure and Transport of Japan, 2008). That specific situation of the construction market as well as the fast increase of takeovers within the construction industry since the mid-nineties poses the question: Do M&A transactions within the construction industry behave differently to the results of the cross-industrial studies? Therefore, I focus my doctoral thesis on the effects of M&A within the construction industry. By applying short-term and long-term analyses, I intend to provide a comprehensive picture of the achieved wealth effects in relation to M&A transactions. Additionally, I show with a specific case that general assumptions about the superior M&A strategy have to be partly revised for acquisitions in the construction industry.

With my analysis I do not only address unanswered aspects within the M&A research, but also try to provide an extensive picture about the advantages and disadvantages of the different M&A strategies within the construction industry for the management of construction and non-construction firms. For construction firms I illuminate whether M&A transactions serve as a remedy to overcome the difficult economic situation and which M&A strategy should be pursued to achieve this goal. For non-construction firms I generally investigate under which circumstances acquisitions of construction firms are worthwhile despite the low profit margins within the construction industry.

1.2 Study One: Objectives and Main Findings

The first study addresses the issue of short-term effects from M&A within the construction industry. Short-term event studies by Delaney and Wamuziri (2004) and Choi and Russel (2004) imply positive wealth effects for the acquirer and the target at acquisitions in the construction industry. However, these studies focus exclusively on the English and the American market respectively. In a global study Pauser et al. (2007) show overall positive wealth effects for the targets and the combined entity of M&A transactions within the construction industry. Nonetheless, the effects for the acquirer remain vague. In addition, none of these studies comprehensively considers the effects of non-construction firms engaging into the construction sector by acquisitions. Furthermore, the development of real estate and construction cycles, which are comprehensively illustrated by Rottke and Wernecke (2002), as a potential factor for the success of the acquisition, is not considered thus far. Therefore, I focus my study on the short-term wealth effects for bidding companies regardless whether the acquirer or the target is a construction firm. I also consider various parameters affecting the transaction success.

By analyzing 354 detected acquisitions in the construction industry in the period from 1985–2004, I find overall positive abnormal returns for the acquiring companies. Nevertheless, non-construction firms yield explicit higher abnormal returns than construction firms. When examining the impact of the strategic focus of the acquisition the results indicate a superiority of horizontal consolidation and vertical integration to lateral diversification for construction firms, which corresponds to findings of Berger and Ofek (1995) and Goergen and Renneboog (2004). Contrarily, industrial non-construction firms achieve higher abnormal returns from conglomerate acquisitions of construction firms than firms integrating vertically construction firms. Similar to the conglomerate acquisitions, financial investors yield high benefits from their engagements in the construction industry.

The result for the geographical orientation of M&A supports for acquisitions by construction firms the findings of Denis et al. (2002) as well as Mentz and Schiereck (2008): Construction firms gain significantly higher abnormal returns for their shareholders on domestic acquisitions than on international diversification. Partly, this superiority results from domestic acquisitions in countries with a real estate boom. For non-construction no clear superior strategy can be determined as acquirers highly gain from domestic and international acquisitions.

Overall, bidders are positively rewarded for their effort to improve their situation within the construction industry or to change market conditions through M&A measures. Hence, the findings from general cross-industrial M&A event studies do not hold true for the construction industry. It rather seems as if the described peculiar situation within the construction industry supports the consolidation and vertical integration process of the construction industry.

1.3 Study Two: Objectives and Main Findings

Although short-term event studies indicate overall positive wealth effects for takeovers within the construction industry, there is no evidence whether the selected M&A strategy remains successful in the long run. Cross-industrial surveys mainly suggest negative wealth impacts for bidders over a period of 12, 24 or 36 months (Rau and Vermaelen, 1998). Nevertheless, as mentioned in the outset, cross-industrial studies often show a high variance in their results implying significant differences among industries (Gregory and McCorriston, 2005). Due to these barriers the partnering research serves as source for setting assumptions for the long-term wealth effects of M&A within the construction industry. Partnering is a common form of cooperation between two or more parties. Crucial aspects of successful partnerships are shared goals, aligned working processes, mutual benefit seeking as well as respect and trust among the involved parties (Lu and Yan, 2007). With partnerships construction firms mainly pursue the goal to bid for large scale and mostly long lasting projects. In addition, construction firms use partnerships to transfer the experienced knowledge of one construction project to the subsequent project, thereby yielding learning effects and reducing the set-up costs at new projects. On the other hand, non-construction firms use partnerships with construction firms in order to obtain high-qualitative construction services from a reliable partner. Overall, the studies on partnering suggest positive effects from these collaborations among the involved parties (Haksever et al., 2001). However, Brensen and Marshall (2000) document that the daily business partnerships often suffer from moral hazard problems and the self-centered interests of partners to abuse the partnership for their own advantages. Therefore, several construction and also non-construction firms prefer a complete acquisition of another firm in order to reach positive wealth effects and to enhance their performance.

When engaging in a M&A transaction the issue concerning the most long-term wealth-creating takeover strategy arises. Acquirers do not only have to consider potential targets themselves, but also markets and their continuously changing conditions to succeed in the long-run. For example, advancements in free trade agreements for construction services enable construction firms to enter new markets more easily. Even though cultural differences and various national laws can be barriers to the market entry, international competition has continued to accelerate during recent years (McGraw-Hill, 2006). On the other hand, the regions develop worldwide differently. For instance, the construction industry within Western Europe only grew slightly from 1996 to 2005 at an average rate of 1.8%. The high levels of public debt in most European countries caused a decline in expenditures of civil engineering projects between 1999 and 2005 (Euroconstruct, 2006). In contrast, the construction volume in most Asian economies has risen steeply since the mid-nineties, which resembles the dynamic development of many Asian economies (Research Institute of Construction and Economy, 2008). Most impressive are the growth rates of the Chinese construction sector. Between 1997 and 2000 the construction industry grew by 10%–12%, but in the period between 2000 and 2005 growth rates rose to 19%–26% and boosted national construction output from 175 to 483 billion USD (National Bureau of Statistics of China, 2008).

For determining whether acquisitions in the construction industry yield positive wealth effects for bidders, I investigate the buy-and-hold abnormal returns (BHAR) for a similar sample as in the short-term event analysis in comparison to reference portfolios consisting of competitors with similar firm characteristics as the acquirers. The received results suggest also for the long run highly positive wealth effects for the bidding companies, which is again in contrast to the documented underperformance of bidding companies in cross-industrial studies (Aggarwal and Samwick, 2003; Rau and Vermaelen, 1998). However, the picture of the results becomes more distinct, when observing the transactions regarding the strategic and geographical focus. Concerning the strategic focus, construction firms benefit clearly more from horizontal acquisitions than from vertical integration, while non-construction firms still achieve the best yields from conglomerate diversification or from using construction firms as financial investments. Only one group reports negative BHAR: Financial institutions or industrial firms that overtake construction firms because of an impending insolvency of the construction firms seem to suffer from saving the construction firm.

The geographical focus shows for construction firms no major impact for the success of the merger even though the domestic takeovers are differentiated into acquisitions in countries with a real estate boom and those without. In both strategies, construction firms gain. Hence, strengthening the business on the home market as well as extending the business into new markets benefits construction firms. However, non-construction firms only benefit from international or domestic acquisitions in real estate booming countries, and suffer performance declines in domestic acquisitions in countries not undergoing a real estate boom.

1.4 Study Three: Objectives and Main Findings

The third study addresses the issue of the adequate M&A strategy for construction firms facing decreasing market volumes on the home market. From most M&A studies I know that horizontal acquisitions with a national focus are superior to other transactions (Denis et al., 2002; Moeller and Schlingemann 2005; Mentz and Schiereck, 2008).The findings from all analyses on the construction industry support the thesis of a superiority of horizontal acquisitions conducted by construction firms. Regarding Anand (2005) the superiority of national and horizontal acquisitions also accounts for M&A transactions in declining markets. I use the case of the German construction firm Walter Bau for examining the appropriateness of the suggested strategy. The firm mainly focused its business and M&A transactions on the highly fragmented German construction market that underwent a severe recession with decreasing market volumes of € 54bn (21%) in the period from 1995–2004 (Statistisches Bundesamt, 2008). I show a detrimental effect on the corporate wealth from the entire M&A strategy regardless whether the target is foreign or domestic. However, I also show that the national acquisitions decreased the corporate value more than the foreign takeovers and might have had an impact on the failure of the company. In contrast to this effect, the depicted benchmarks of the case seemed to benefit from their strategy to distribute their operations to other countries as well as to sectors other than the original construction business. The only consistent successful business unit of the observed construction firm stresses this assumption, as it generates its revenues abroad by providing technical solutions and equipment for complex civil engineering projects. Thus, focusing on the home market with horizontal acquisitions seems an inferior strategy in declining markets that are also highly fragmented like the construction industry.

2 Consolidation, Value Chain Extension and Outside Industry Investors – Value-Generating M&A Strategies in the Construction Industry

Abstract

The construction industry belongs – with a share of 10% of the global GDP – to the biggest industry sectors worldwide but faces serious challenges due to strong price competition, small profit margins and a highly fragmented market. To overcome these challenges, several construction companies intend to augment their market power by conducting Mergers and Acquisitions (M&A). In addition, many construction firms become a takeover target by firms from outside the construction industry.

This study examines, on the one hand, the value effects for construction firms when engaging in M&A. On the other hand, it surveys the wealth effects for non-construction firms when purchasing construction companies. Overall, the results suggest that these takeovers are beneficial for the bidder shareholders. However, the wealth benefits depend strongly on the strategic and geographical focus as well as the general stock market developments. Profitability and growth expectations of the bidder firm account for further relevant success factors.

2.1 Introduction

Now, more than ever, the construction industry faces numerous challenges on a global and local scale (Rice, 2007). The complexity of most construction projects poses high operational and financial risks. Construction companies can only approximate these risks, because most projects are unique, vary in size and characteristics and require always a project-specific monitoring, since the constellation of subcontractors usually differs (Black et al., 2000). The risks inherent to construction projects can be transferred only to a certain extent to subcontractors or even the project principal due to the tense competition for projects (Construction Industry Federation, 2007).

The accelerating pace of globalization and the interdependency of international markets even further increase competition between construction companies. The general challenges are accompanied by the recession on the American housing market since 2007 and a decline by 2.5% in the overall American construction production (Deutsche Bank Research, 2008). Likewise, the growth expectations for the construction volume on the European market turned negative in 2008 for the first time since 2002 (Euroconstruct, 2008). Due to these challenges, construction firms have to adapt their business strategy to strengthen their market position and to be able to successfully compete within the global construction market. As one consequence, numerous construction companies have undergone acquisition activities – in the period 1995-2006 there was a total increase of approximately 230% compared to the previous decade – to overcome the insecure economic situation (Rice, 2007).

A major motive of takeovers is to achieve operative synergies through economies of scale or scope (Berkovitch and Narayanan, 1993; Goergen and Renneboog, 2004). Furthermore, the size of a construction company often determines the perceived competence and the reliability to accomplish complex construction projects. Therefore, construction companies try to enhance their business growth and reputation by initiating horizontal takeovers (Delaney and Wamuziri, 2004). Purchasing a competitor does not only raise the company's size, but also provides several further advantages for the acquirer. First, a takeover of a competitor often turns out to be less expensive than endogenous growth. Second, competitors vanish from the market, thereby increasing the market share of the acquirer (Green and Cromley 1982). Nevertheless, Eckbo (1982) argues that the remaining competitors do not suffer from the takeover but rather benefit from the market concentration. Third, takeovers reduce significantly the firm's income and survival risk (Amihud et al., 1986).

Furthermore, horizontal acquisitions entail stronger market power of the acquirer, enabling companies to strengthen their position with customers (Lewellen, 1971). For example, from the merger between the Spanish construction companies Actividades de Construccion y Servicios (ACS) and Dragados y

Construcciones in 2003 emerged one of the biggest construction companies in Europe and one of the top ten in the world measured by sales (ACS, 2004). Regarding Gort (1969) and Levin/Peck (2003), companies engaging in horizontal acquisitions even endeavour to obtain oligopoly or monopoly market power. Such a scenario will most probably not occur at the construction industry within the near future due to the current low level of market concentration (Euroconstruct, 2007; Engineering News Record, 2005).

Vertical takeovers focus on enlarging the value chain by the acquisition of businesses that are situated upstream or downstream from the firm's original business (Green and Cromley, 1982). By this means, the corporation incorporates supply and distribution channels and obtains the opportunity to allocate its resources more efficiently (Jensen, 1983). Laussel (2008) contradicts these benefits for upstream acquisitions as prices of pre-products by the remaining subcontractors increases, which could have an offsetting or even negative impact for the bidder. However, the author focuses on a model with a monopolistic downstream firm and refers to the manufacturing industry with standardized production processes. The construction industry is a project-oriented industry with lower standardization level of the working processes than the manufacturing industry (Black et al., 2000). Even though efficiency gains can be realized by long-term cooperation, the general contractor relies less on its subcontractors and can easily switch between those at each project. Therefore, the negative aspects of backward integration described by Laussel (2008) could be more moderate within the construction industry. Downstream acquisitions refer, for instance, to the purchase of real estate operations companies. Unlike the original construction services, real estate operations ensure mid- or even long-term steady and safe cash flows for the company and reduce the risk of volatile earnings. In 2003 Grupo Ferrovial a Spanish construction firm offering various kinds of construction services including airport construction used this type of takeover to enlarge its value chain by purchasing the Belfast City Airport, an English airport operator (Thomson Financial, 2008). In vertical takeovers construction firms also integrate the necessary knowledge to offer complete solution projects. Especially Public Private Partnership (PPP) projects require the capabilities to design, develop, finance, build, operate and maintain public institutions.[1]

Besides the horizontal and vertical options, some construction enterprises intend to increase the firm value by purchasing companies from business sectors other than construction. Nonetheless, often a construction firm can use the ac-

1 PPP projects were originally developed because of the financial bottlenecks of public institutions. In these projects, the private construction firm does not only finance and build the public facility but also operates the facility. In return, the public institution does not settle at once the entire construction cost but pays an annuity to the construction firm over a predetermined period.

quired business in a certain manner for its construction services like transportation service (e.g. in 2002 the Peterhouse Group, an English residential builder, overtook First Engineering Holdings, a transportation company). Still, those conglomerate takeovers tend to diversify the business fields to become more independent from a single revenue stream thereby diminishing the risk of failure (Green and Cromley, 1982). In spite of these positive intended goals, conglomerate extension often entails negative wealth effects. For instance, Berger and Ofek (1995) report a discount of -13% to -15% for conglomerate diversification. Hence, conglomerate diversification can also cause wealth hazards for shareholders.

On the other hand several construction companies have become a takeover target by bidders from other industries. In around 76.3% of the cases, the bidders come from construction-related businesses and tend to extend their value chain vertically by purchasing a construction company. (For example, in 2004, Balfour Betty, an English real estate developer, bought Gammon Skanska, a residency constructor [Thomson Financial, 2008].) A further 18.3% of the bidders are not directly linked to the construction business but acquire construction businesses to internalize construction service into their company or simply to extent their business scope. The remaining 5.4% of the takeovers result from financial problems of the construction firm. The contractor buys the construction firm to avoid a cancellation of the project.

Financial instability of construction firms causes even 17% of the takeovers by financial firms. Financial firms engage in these acquisitions to prevent a failure of the construction firm and hence a loss of their provided loans. For example in 1996 the Royal Bank of Scotland acquired the Charles Church Group, a residency constructor that was close to bankruptcy to avert a depreciation of the provided loans. Nevertheless, financial investments reasons account for the major part (83%) of the acquisitions of construction firms. Mainly, real estate investment trusts (REITs) and private equity funds use acquisitions of construction firms in order to diversify their investment portfolio (Thomson Financial, 2008).

Even though a consolidation of the construction industry is essential for its firms, the shareholders still face the risk that managers pursue their personal advantage by increasing their personal portfolio instead of acting in favour of the shareholder interests (Aggarwal and Samwick, 2003). Sometimes managers engage in value-destroying takeover activities, as they are too overconfident in their capabilities and overestimate the benefits of the acquisition. Roll (1986) describes this behaviour as hubris. Similar to this motive is the irrationality of managers to use excess cash flow for the takeover of poor-performing enterprises (Jensen, 1986). Managers also enjoy higher reputation and remuneration from running a big-size company (Jensen and Murphy, 1990; Stulz, 1990). If managers are in charge of a big-size company, in particular of highly diversified enterprises with interwoven subdivisions, they will become more indispensable for their principals, as they dispose of the required knowledge to run the company (Shleifer and Vishny, 1989). Therefore, acquisitions and increasing firm size can cause a financial trade-off for the business owners and does not necessarily mean an increase in economic wealth for its shareholders.

Next to the several strategic focuses of the acquisitions, several construction companies enlarge their operations by international diversification. International transactions enable construction enterprises to compete on a global scale and to satisfy the demands of international customers. Furthermore, it diversifies the earning streams to various countries and reduces the dependency on a single market and consequently diminishes the risk of volatile earnings that can be caused by economic recession in domestic markets (Eun et al., 1996). For instance, in 2006 HOCHTIEF, a leading construction firm based in Germany, suffered a loss from its original construction business in Europe. However, these losses were counterbalanced by gains from the company's overseas businesses (HOCHTIEF, 2007).

In spite of this development and the magnitude of the construction industry – approximately 10% of global GDP steams from construction activities (McGraw-Hill Construction, 2006) – there has been limited capital market research about the benefits and effects of M&A activities within the construction industry. The studies investigating the wealth effects from M&A within the construction firm remain constrained in implications for shareholder of the acquiring companies, particularly when those are involved into international takeovers.

Based on the already accomplished findings, the research intention is manifold. I first try to illuminate the direct wealth effects for construction bidding firms announcing a takeover. Furthermore, I investigate the value effects for non-construction firms announcing a takeover of a construction company. If M&A within the construction industry create shareholder value for the acquiring company, it might serve as a valuable option to leave the above mentioned economic dilemma. Additionally, a detailed regression analysis highlights the relevant factors affecting the value creation (or even destruction) resulting from the analyzed acquisitions.

The study is organized as follows. Current research in the field is reviewed, including the necessity for a more comprehensive survey about M&A within the construction industry. Afterward I examine comprehensively the value effects and success factors of M&A transactions within the construction. Finally, the results of this research are interpreted and the major findings highlighted.

2.2 Related Literatures

Ample research has been conducted on the wealth effect of M&A activities. However, most studies do not concentrate on one single industry, but instead use M&A from various industry sectors for their surveys. The reported results commonly reveal positive significant abnormal returns for the targets (Jensen and

Ruback, 1983; Andrade et al., 2001; Jovanovic and Barguinsky, 2004). Andrade et al. (2001) scrutinize 1,864 mergers between 1973 and 1998. They detect remarkable abnormal returns for the targets. Within an event window of [-1;1], the targets accomplished cumulated average abnormal returns (CAAR) of 15.9%. When the event window is enlarged to [-20;20] the CAAR rose to 23.3%. These results are all significant at a level of 1%.

In contrast there is no consistent picture of the wealth effects for the shareholders of the bidding companies. Recent research predominantly provides evidence for the negative or no impact of M&A on the shareholder value of bidding firms. Bruner (2002), Campa and Hernando (2004 and 2006), Moeller et al. (2005) and Swanstrom (2006) all report negative or zero cumulated average abnormal returns (CAAR) for shareholders of bidder companies. Eckbo and Thorburn (2000) find abnormal returns that are slightly positive for bidders, whereas the results were only positive for international and non-domestic takeovers. Moeller et al. (2004) also detect positive bidder CAAR, which, however, become negative when weighted by market capitalization. Other studies ascertain both negative and positive results for the bidders (Dodd, 1980; Asquith, 1983) or display no effect at all on the shareholder wealth due to M&A activities (Franks and Harris, 1989).

Within the construction sector, three studies have analyzed so far the shareholder wealth effects attributed to M&A activities. Delaney and Wamuziri (2004) detect high positive abnormal returns for acquirers and targets in domestic takeovers within the UK. While the 20.9% CAAR for the targets at the 41-day event window around the announcement of the M&A transaction coincide with the cross-industry findings of Andrade et al. (2001), 8.19% of the acquiring firms outperform all cross-industry results from the recent studies. However, the analyzed sample is small, concentrates on one specific country, includes firms from the construction material industry and does not distinguish between the effects for both sectors. Similar constraints account for the domestic M&A study within the construction industry by Choi and Russel (2004). They concentrate on acquiring US firms and report an insignificant CAAR of 2.41% over the 41-day event window. Subsequently, the interpretation of the findings of these two analyses remains rather vague.

Pauser et al. (2007) investigate 106 takeovers in the construction industry on a global scale over the period 1986–2006. The acquirer sample consists exclusively of construction companies, while the target panel contains construction and non-construction businesses. The CAAR of the announced acquisitions display shareholder value generation and positive abnormal returns through M&A activities. In line with cross-industry studies, particularly the target firm shareholders enjoy a CAAR of 20.98% at the 41-day event window. The shareholders of the bidder firms also accomplished an insignificant positive CAAR of 1.35% for the same period, which confirms the results of the previous two studies for takeovers in the construction industry. The CAAR for the value-weighted combined entity of bidder and target amounts to 3.11%.

The results are also positive for three different time periods (1986–1992, 1993–1999, 2000–2006), for the major industrial regions (Europe, North America and Asia) and for the horizontal, vertical and conglomerate strategic focuses. Furthermore, while vertical takeovers depict positive CAAR, conglomerate acquisitions seem to destroy shareholder value. The positive synergy effects for shareholders of acquiring companies also cannot be supported, since the horizontal CAAR show positive and negative abnormal returns. All results for the acquirer are insignificant. Thus, extending the value chain seems to be the dominant strategy in the construction industry.

Although all three studies indicate a tendency towards positive wealth effects for bidding construction firms from M&A activities none demonstrates any significant results and a comprehensive disclosure about the wealth effects for the acquirers. Moreover, to the authors' best knowledge the issue of non-construction firms purchasing a construction company has not been examined so far. Therefore, this study shall not only contribute comprehensive insight into the wealth effects of bidding construction companies, but also for takeovers of the opposite direction.

The wealth effects for the targets are not addressed in this study, since the existing studies describe extensive abnormal returns for the targets. The financial literature attributes the abnormal target returns to the free-rider phenomenon in public tender offers and the agency problematic. The agency problematic anticipates high returns for the shareholders of the target firms, since the integration of a badly managed firm into a well-managed acquirer entails positive expectations on future returns (Grossmann and Hart, 1980; Jensen 1986). Hence, the contribution of another study demonstrating high CAAR for target shareholders would be negligible.

2.3 Data and Methodology

2.3.1 Data and Sample Selection

I determine the construction companies regarding the standard industrial code scheme (SIC), which is closely related to the industry classification of the United Nations (ISIC F-45). The relevant SIC for the construction industry refer to the digits 1500–1799. The investigation focuses on the stock market reactions of bidding firms in M&A activities. This comprises construction companies purchasing another company on a vertical, horizontal or conglomerate basis. This also includes the value effects for non-construction companies buying a construction company. The latter group is divided into industrial companies and financial investors. As a reference date for the M&A event itself, the literature proves that the announcement day of the takeover is the most adequate (Fama et al., 1969).

I retrieved 12,199 transactions from the Thomson One Banker database within the period 1982 to 2004. From this initial panel only the transactions are included, which comply with the following criteria:

1. The acquiring firm must have been listed on a public stock exchange for at least the 252 days before the takeover announcement.
2. The transaction must be completed.
3. The transaction volume must equal or exceed an amount of 20 million USD.
4. The bidding firm must gain control of the target (at least 50% + 1 share)

After applying these criteria, 354 transactions remain for the analysis: 243 transactions are initiated by construction companies acquiring another construction firm or an unrelated business and 111 bidders are non-construction firms purchasing a construction company. Table 2.1 provides an overview about some characteristics of the takeovers:

Table 2.1: Sample Overview

Year	N	Horizontal	Vertical	Conglo-merate	Industrial non-construction firms	Financial Firms	Cross border	Total Transaction Volume (mn USD)	Avergage Transaction Volume (mn USD)
2004	17	4	7	2	3	1	1	1,514.19	89.07
2003	33	16	6	2	6	3	9	8,193.60	248.29
2002	50	25	8	3	12	2	12	8,092.48	161.85
2001	42	18	6	5	13	0	12	8,410.09	200.24
2000	57	23	8	11	12	3	22	11,520.30	202.11
1999	40	11	7	9	10	3	13	12,053.78	301.34
1998	37	15	10	2	9	1	5	4,580.05	123.79
1997	12	7	1	1	3	0	2	4,335.11	361.26
1996	21	4	7	1	7	2	7	3,310.20	157.63
1995	13	7	0	1	4	1	5	1,196.43	96.20
1994	10	2	3	0	5	0	3	583.05	58.30
1993	1	1	0	0	0	0	0	34.52	34.52
1992	3	3	0	0	0	0	0	128.99	43.00
1991	3	0	0	1	2	0	0	3,320.74	1,106.91
1990	6	1	1	0	4	0	0	2,188.00	364.67
1989	4	0	1	1	1	1	1	1,520.26	380.07
1988	2	0	1	0	1	0	1	81.56	40.78
1987	2	0	1	0	0	1	0	82.22	41.11
1986	0	0	0	0	0	0	0	0.00	0.00
1985	1	0	0	0	1	0	1	445.00	445.00
Σ	**354**	**137**	**67**	**39**	**93**	**18**	**94**	**71,591.00**	**222.81**

Table 2.1 illustrates 354 takeovers, in which construction firms are involved either as bidders or targets in the period 1985–2004. The construction bidder sample is subdivided into its dif-

ferent strategic focuses. The non-construction bidders are subdivided into industrial and financial firms. The cross-border section refers to the international acquisition and the total transaction volume to the cumulated transaction volume of all bidders within one year. The high average transaction volumes in the years 1989, 1990 and 1991 result from the small number of identified acquisition complying with the selection criteria. In addition, in 1991 the English conglomerate Hanson PLC bought Beazer PLC, one of the biggest residential constructor and producer of constructing aggregates in the US, for nearly 3 bn USD (Thomson Financial, 2008; Austin, 1992).

2.3.2 Methodology

The used stock data refers to the total stock return of each company. Using the total stock return permits a consistent analysis of the bidders' performance. Within the event study I apply the market model approach regarding Brown and Warner (1985) for analyzing the wealth effects due to M&A:

$$\overline{R}_{i,t} = \overline{\alpha}_i + \overline{\beta}_i * \overline{R}_{m,t}$$

$\overline{R}_{i,t}$ refers to the expected return of the stock derived from the estimation period of 252 trading days before the event window. $\overline{R}_{m,t}$ illustrates the return of the market portfolio within the estimation period. The variable $\overline{\alpha}_i$ is the part of the stock return that is independent from the market return. The coefficient $\overline{\beta}_i$ defines the impact of the market return on the stock return i. Due to the possibility of no synchronous or thin trading of shares, the derived beta values by the OLS method can be biased (Scholes and Williams, 1977). Therefore, the beta values are adjusted regarding the method of McInish and Wood (1986). The abnormal stock return is determined by subtracting the estimated stock returns from the actual returns ($R_{i,t}$) of the event window:

$$AR_{i,t} = R_{i,t} - \overline{R}_{i,t}$$

The cumulated abnormal return for each firm is determined by the sum of all abnormal returns of the period of the event window:

$$CAR_{i,[t,T]} = \sum_{t=1}^{T} AR_{i,t}$$

To receive the cumulated average abnormal returns of all stocks, all cumulate abnormal stock returns are averaged:

$$CAAR_{i,[t,T]} = \frac{1}{N} \sum_{t=1}^{T} CAR_{i,t}$$

The significance of the results is tested with the parametric Boehmer test (Boehmer et al., 1991) as well as the non-parametric Wilcoxon-signed-rank-test (MacKinlay, 1997).

2.4 Empirical Results

In this section I discuss the major findings of the empirical analysis. The chapter is organized as follows. In section 2.4.1 I depict the overall wealth effects for bidding firms involved in M&A transactions in the construction industry. The overall analysis is composed of a comparison of differences in performance for all construction and non-construction bidders. In the subsequent sections of chapter 2.4.1 I illustrate the takeover announcement effects for various sub-groups. Afterward, the strategic focuses of M&A are analyzed in detail. As internalization becomes increasingly relevant for any business, the value effects for shareholders of international transactions in comparison to domestic acquisitions are demonstrated. Finally, the analysis reviews the bidder abnormal returns of 1985–1992, 1993–1999 and the first five years of the new millennium.

2.4.1 Overall Sample Analysis

Figure 2.1 depicts the CAAR of all 354 bidders for the period of -20 days before until 20 days after the takeover announcement:

Figure 2.1: CAAR Overview of All Bidders

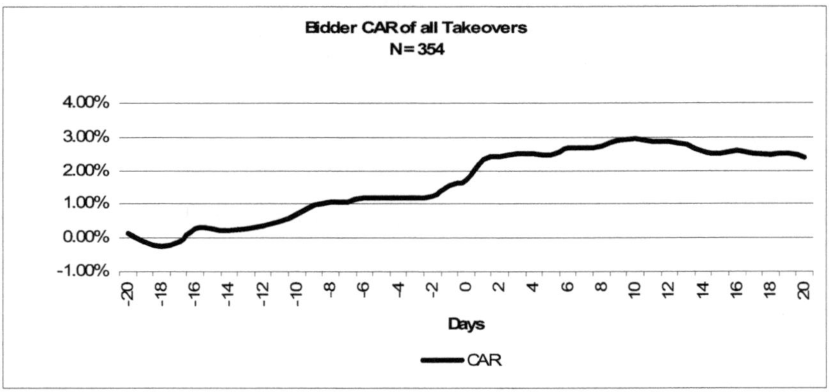

Figure 2.1 illustrates the average CAR development around the announcement date of acquisitions, in which the construction firms are either involved in as bidders or targets.

As the figure displays, bidding firms achieve substantial wealth effects from takeovers. Most of the value increase occurs exactly around the announcement day. The highest growth rate in CAAR is documented for the day after the announcement (0.61% abnormal return rise). Thus the capital market immediately reacts to the takeover announcement. The CAAR achievements before the announcement day also seem remarkable. The average of the 354 firms has already accomplished nearly 50% of the CAAR gains two days before the announcement day. This phenomenon results from merger speculation or information leakage that leads to abnormal stock price movements prior to the transaction announcement. A numerical overview of the wealth effects is provided in the following table:

Table 2.2: CAAR of All Bidders

Overall Sample Analysis; N=354							
Event Window	CAAR	Boehmer test (t-value)	Median	Wilcoxon (z-score)	Min-Value	Max-Value	Positives
[-20,+20]	2.34%	2.822***	1.82%	-2.418**	-66.56%	67.66%	53.67%
[-10,+10]	2.41%	3.995***	2.41%	-3.793***	-35.48%	59.95%	56.78%
[-5;+5]	1.27%	2.695***	0.41%	-2.263**	-32.63%	34.59%	52.82%
[-1,+1]	1.09%	3.651***	0.69%	-2.418**	-17.36%	27.83%	57.34%

Table 2.2 illustrates the average and medians of the cumulated abnormal returns of 354 quoted acquirer firms worldwide that conducted a M&A transaction within the construction industry in the period from 1985 until 2004. *, **, *** indicate the statistical significance to the 10%, 5% and 1% levels, respectively. The Min-Value refers to the company with the lowest abnormal returns resulting from the takeover. The Max-Value refers to the company with the highest abnormal returns resulting from the takeover. The Positive-Value refers to the percentage of takeovers with positive abnormal returns.

The CAAR of the event window [-1;1] report with 1.09% the lowest CAAR. The event window [-10;10] documents with 2.41% the highest CAAR for the bidders and the longest event window of [-20;20] lies slightly below the 21-day event window with a CAAR rate of 2.34%. This implies that the capital market prices in the predominant part of the takeover effects in the [-10;10] event window. The p-values indicate overall significant results on the 1% level. The highest achieved abnormal returns amount to 67.66% and the lowest to -66.56% within the 41-day event window for a single company. The median values of 0.69% of the [-1;1] and of 1.82% of the [-20;20] event window are slightly lower, while the results for the [-10;10] event window correspond to the respective CAAR. Not surprisingly, only the latter result is significant at the 1% level regarding the Wilcoxon-Signed-Rank test, while the remaining results are only significant at the 5% level. The significant results imply that the mean of M&A within the construction industry create additional wealth to the shareholders of bidding firms. When dividing the overall sample into construction and non-construction firms the positive picture remains significantly positive for both groups but becomes more distinct:

Table 2.3: CAAR of Construction Firms and Non-Construction Firms

Construction Firms; N=243				
Event Window	[-20,+20]	[-10,+10]	[-5;+5]	[-1,+1]
CAAR	1.91%**	2.11%***	1.08%*	0.9%***
Median	2.04%*	2.71%***	0.36%	0.59%***
Min-Value	-51.40%	-27.39%	-32.63%	-16.80%
Max-Value	60.79%	37.93%	34.04%	18.96%
Positive	53.50%	55.97%	51.85%	57.61%
Non-Construction Firms; N=111				
Event Window	[-20,+20]	[-10,+10]	[-5;+5]	[-1,+1]
CAAR	3.34%**	3.12%**	1.7%*	1.5%**
Median	1.67%	1.84%**	1.84%	0.79%**
Min-Value	-66.56%	-35.48%	-25.25%	-17.36%
Max-Value	67.66%	59.95%	34.59%	27.83%
Positive	54.05%	58.56%	54.95%	56.76%
Difference Test				
Mean: t-value	-0.793	-0.765	-0.605	-0.963
Median: z-score	0.232	0.364	0.638	0.512

Table 2.3 illustrates the average and medians of the cumulated abnormal returns of 243 quoted construction acquirer firms as well as 111 quoted non-construction firms worldwide that were involved as bidders in takeovers within the construction industry in the period from 1985 until 2004. *, **, *** indicate the statistical significance to the 10%, 5% and 1% levels, respectively. The significance for the CAAR and median values is tested with Boehmer test and the Wilcoxon-Signed-Rank, respectively. The Min-Value refers to the company with the lowest abnormal returns resulting from the horizontal takeover. The Max-Value refers to the company with the highest abnormal returns resulting from the horizontal takeover. The Positive-Value refers to the percentage of takeovers with positive abnormal returns.

The sample of the non-construction firms outperforms the construction firms on all event windows. This also accounts for the percentage of firms accomplishing positive abnormal returns apart from the [-1;1] event window. The best-performing non-construction firm also exceeds with its highest abnormal return the best performing construction firm by almost 7% on the [-20;20] event window. Even more noticeable is the gap at the [-10;10] event window. Here, the surplus of the most successful non-construction to its construction counterpart amounts to slightly more than 22%. However, the differences between the two groups are not significant. On the other hand, the worst-performing construction enterprise suffers from ca. -51.40% negative abnormal return, but the analogous non-construction firm records nearly -66.56%. It seems that the shareholders of non-construction firms may generally enjoy higher abnormal returns, but also have to fear big discounts from conglomerate diversification of their companies. Likewise to the owners of non-construction enterprises, shareholders of construction firms benefit from takeovers affirming the findings of Pauser et al.

(2007). The subsequent analysis serves to uncover the variances in the wealth effects from the diverse acquisition strategies.

2.4.2 Strategic Focuses of Takeovers

As can be derived from Table 2.4, bidders gain significant abnormal returns when purchasing a competitor. Although the wealth effect is on the [-1;1] event window with 1.1% still low, the CAAR steadily increase to 1.69%, 2.16% and 2.88% of the [-5;5], [-10;10] and [-20;20] event windows, respectively. All CAAR prove to be significant on the 5% level. The results from the median analysis diverge to a small degree from the CAAR, but mainly confirm the bidder gains in horizontal takeovers. The results correspond to the assumption that construction companies yield high synergies from mergers and acquisitions of competitors. Since the original business of the acquirer is enlarged at horizontal takeovers, the crucial factor "business size" is enhanced (chapter 2.1).

Vertical takeovers show small abnormal returns for the bidders at the [-1;1] event window the CAAR (0.53%) and the median (0.85%). Neither of these results is significant. If the observation is enlarged to the [-10;10] event window, the CAAR rises to a percentage of 3.34% and the median to 3.37%. Now the CAAR are significant at the 1% level and the median at the 5% level. However, on the [-20;20] event window the CAAR and median values drop a little to 2.51% and 2.32% respectively. These results are only significant on the 10% level. Although the upward tendency does not sustain over all event windows, the results overall indicate positive wealth effects from vertical takeovers. The capital market recognizes positively the enlargement of the value chain to other construction or real estate services and the extension to less volatile revenue streams. Furthermore, the purchase of upstream and especially downstream businesses raises the level of technical competence as well as the size of the construction company, thereby improving its competitive strength. The benefits from a value chain extension within the construction industry are perfectly in line with the report of the English Construction Task Force. They stress in a report a strong need for construction firms to raise the efficiency of their supply chain network for avoiding exorbitant costs (Egan, 1998).

If construction companies extend their business to unrelated business fields through M&A, they apparently destroy shareholder value as assumed. The CAAR and median values are slightly above zero (0.83% and 0.45%) at the [-1;1] event window, but at the remaining three event windows the calculated abnormal returns turn negative. Hence, the CAAR and median values of -2.47% and -2.10% at the 41-day event period strengthens the assumption of destructive conglomerate M&A activities, although none of the CAAR and median values are significant. The positive abnormal returns at horizontal and vertical takeovers and the negative impact on shareholder wealth at conglomerate diversification strongly support the statement of Singh and Montgomery (1987) that related acquisitions are expected to achieve higher benefits and lower integration costs than unrelated acquisitions.

Table 2.4: CAAR of Horizontal, Vertical and Conglomerate Takeovers by Construction Firms

Horizontal Takeovers; N=137				
Event Window	[-20,+20]	[-10,+10]	[-5;+5]	[-1,+1]
CAAR	2.88%**	2.16%**	1.69%**	1.1%**
Median	2.67%**	2.78%**	0.81%**	0.63%**
Min-Value	-51.40%	-27.39%	-20.32%	-16.80%
Max-Value	60.79%	37.93%	32.24%	16.78%
Positive	54.74%	58.39%	52.55%	59.85%
Vertical Takeovers; N=67				
Event Window	[-20,+20]	[-10,+10]	[-5;+5]	[-1,+1]
CAAR	2.51%*	3.34%***	1.21%	0.53%
Median	3.2%*	3.37%**	0.47%	0.85%
Min-Value	-26.24%	-17.67%	-22.18%	-16.19%
Max-Value	29.42%	29.45%	34.04%	12.10%
Positive	58.21%	61.19%	59.70%	56.72%
Conglomerate Takeovers; N=39				
Event Window	[-20,+20]	[-10,+10]	[-5;+5]	[-1,+1]
CAAR	-2.47%	-0.11%	-1.26%	0.83%
Median	-2.10%	-1.62%	-2.05%	0.45%
Min-Value	-36.74%	-24.10%	-32.63%	-7.41%
Max-Value	43.70%	27.84%	24.10%	18.96%
Positive	43.59%	41.03%	38.46%	53.85%
Difference Test; Horizontal - Vertical				
Mean: t-value	0.167	0.726	-0.388	-0.714
Median: z-score	0.119	0.636	-0.258	-0.568
Difference Test; Horizontal - Conglomerate				
Mean: t-value	1.849*	1.124*	1.920*	0.275
Median: z-score	-2.045**	-1.307	-1.916*	-0.801
Difference Test; Vertical - Conglomerate				
Mean: t-value	1.835*	1.767*	1.371	-0.299
Median: z-score	-2.015**	-1.831*	-1.569	-0.383

Table 2.4 illustrates the average and medians of the cumulated abnormal returns of 243 quoted construction acquirer firms worldwide that conducted a horizontal, vertical or conglomerate M&A transaction in the period from 1985 until 2004. *, **, *** indicate the statistical significance to the 10%, 5% and 1% levels, respectively. The significance for the CAAR and median values is tested with Boehmer test and the Wilcoxon-Signed-Rank, respectively. The Min-Value refers to the company with the lowest abnormal returns resulting from the horizontal takeover. The Max-Value refers to the company with the highest abnormal returns

resulting from the horizontal takeover. The Positive-Value refers to the percentage of takeovers with positive abnormal returns.

In contrast to the findings from conglomerate takeovers, the CAAR and median are consistent and remarkable above zero when the bidder is a non-construction firm and announces a takeover of a construction firm. The abnormal returns increase with the enlargement of the event windows. At the 3-day event period, the CAAR values amount to 1.33% but nearly triple to 3.6% at the 21-day period. All CAAR values of the 3- to 21-day observation period are at least significant at the 5% level. Thus, it seems as if the capital market becomes steadily more convinced from the success of the acquisition of construction firms even though the CAAR levels off to 2.46% of the 41-day observation period, which is, however, not significant.

Table 2.5: Detailed CAAR Analysis of Takeovers by Non-Construction Firms

Non-Construction Firms excluding Financial Firms; N=93				
Event Window	[-20,+20]	[-10,+10]	[-5;+5]	[-1,+1]
CAAR	2.46%	3.60%***	2.03%**	1.33%**
Median	1.31%	3.02%***	1.14%*	0.78%*
Min-Value	-66.56%	-35.48%	-25.25%	-17.36%
Max-Value	55.20%	59.95%	34.59%	27.83%
Positive	53.76%	59.14%	55.91%	55.91%
Financial Firms; N=18				
Event Window	[-20,+20]	[-10,+10]	[-5,+5]	[-1,+1]
CAAR	7.85%	0.79%	1.59%	2.50%
Median	2.87%	0.14%	0.85%	2.78%
Min-Value	-16.56%	-18.72%	-18.15%	-11.34%
Max-Value	67.66%	33.93%	17.41%	22.88%
Positive	55.56%	55.56%	50.00%	61.11%
Difference Test				
Mean: t-value	0.232	0.364	0.638	0.512
Median: z-score	0.084	0.000	-0.676	0.748

Table 2.5 illustrates the average and medians of the cumulated abnormal returns of 111 quoted non-construction firms worldwide that purchased a construction firm in the period from 1985 until 2004. *, **, *** indicate the statistical significance to the 10%, 5% and 1% levels, respectively, applying the Boehmer test at the CAAR values and the Wilcoxon-Signed-Rank test at the median values. The Min-Value refers to the company with the lowest abnormal returns resulting from the takeover. The Max-Value refers to the company with the highest abnormal returns resulting from the takeover. The Positive-Value refers to the percentage of takeovers with positive abnormal returns.

The CAAR of financial investors absorbing a construction company shows an inconsistent development. At the [-1;1] event window, the CAAR amounts to 2.5%, then drops to 1.59% at the [-5;5] and even to 0.79% at the [-10;10] event window and finally escalates to 7.85% at the 41-day observation period. The median fluctuates from 2.78% to 0.85%, 0.14% and then to 2.87% at the respective event windows. Due to the small number of observations and the resulting insignificant results, no reliable implications can be drawn for the value effects for financial investors when overtaking a construction firm. In total, the results imply positive wealth effects for financial firms at M&A activities in the construction industry. Nevertheless, if differentiating the takeovers of non-construction firms regarding their strategic reasons, conglomerate extensions as well as financial investments by REITs or private equity firms seem to be the highly successful transactions for the bidders.

Table 2.6: CAAR of Vertical and Conglomerate Takeovers by Non-Construction Firms

Vertical Takeovers; N=71				
Event Window	[-20,+20]	[-10,+10]	[-5;+5]	[-1,+1]
CAAR	1.26%	2.41%	1.13%	0.69%
Median	0.58%	1.10%	0.64%	0.49%
Min-Value	-66.56%	-35.48%	-25.25%	-17.36%
Max-Value	55.20%	59.95%	34.59%	18.20%
Positive	52.11%	53.52%	52.11%	52.11%
Conglomerate Takeovers; N=17				
Event Window	[-20,+20]	[-10,+10]	[-5,+5]	[-1,+1]
CAAR	7.28%*	6.80%**	4.60%*	3.67%*
Median	8.48%*	7.49%**	2.14%*	1.35%**
Min-Value	-15.56%	-9.36%	-7.49%	-4.90%
Max-Value	41.10%	31.88%	26.22%	27.83%
Positive	54.05%	58.56%	54.95%	56.76%
Difference Test				
Mean: t-value	-1.418	-1.277	-1.302	-1.772*
Median: z-score	1.311	1.849*	1.289	1.722*

Table 2.6 illustrates the average and medians of the cumulated abnormal returns of 88 takeovers by non-construction firms worldwide that either extended their value chain by a vertical acquisition or diversified their business by a conglomerate takeover of a constructions firm in the period from 1985 until 2004. *, **, *** indicate the statistical significance to the 10%, 5% and 1% level, respectively, applying the Boehmer test at the CAAR values and the Wilcoxon-Signed-Rank test at the median values. The Min-Value refers to the company with the lowest abnormal returns resulting from the takeover. The Max-Value refers to the company with the highest abnormal returns resulting from the takeover. The Positive-Value refers to the percentage of takeovers with positive abnormal returns.

The results depict steady positive abnormal returns for non-construction firms extending their value chain or diversifying their business into the construction industry. However, while the gains for vertical acquisitions remain rather low (CAAR value on the 41-day event window: 1.26%), conglomerate acquisitions accomplish high positive abnormal returns over all four event windows (CAAR value on the 41-day event window: 7.28%). Although the sample of conglomerate acquisitions is only composed of 17 acquisitions, the achieved CAAR values are all significant at least on the 10% level. The positive findings on conglomerate takeovers contradict recent literature on diversification but back the arguments in favor of diversification. These positive effects might stem from the avoidance of information asymmetries at construction projects when internalizing construction services (Stein, 1997). Hence, companies that regularly require construction services might benefit from having a construction department within their company instead of purchasing the services over the market. Besides, the integration of construction services permits an improved surveillance of the project quality. Often, the construction costs can be reduced by having incorporated construction services. These aspects can especially become relevant during real estate "up-cycles". Rottke and Wernecke (2002) state that within those "up-cycles" construction firms notice a high demand for construction services. This commonly leads to higher prices for construction services. Additionally, construction firms often accept too many contracts in order to benefit from the current high demand as much as possible. As a consequence, the quality of the construction projects often declines and can cause elementary difficulties for the customer. For example, a facility manager might face the challenge to lease the object profitably. Consequently, an acquisition of a construction firm prevents these moral hazard problems for the acquirer and contributes positively to the corporate wealth.

Financial firms using the acquisition of construction firm as a financial investment accomplish positive abnormal returns around the announcement date of the takeover. The CAAR values of those transactions oscillate over the various event windows from a low CAAR value of 0.62% at the 11-day event window up to 8.31% at the 41-day event window. Despite this inconsistency, the positive CAAR values support in general acquisition activities of financial firms within the construction firm. Even non-construction firms and banks purchasing a construction company due to its financial difficulties seem to win rather than to lose on such deals. Therefore, the avoidance of the failure and the subsequent depreciation of a construction project or the provided loans to the construction firm outweigh the acquired "financial instability". In addition, the financial difficulties make construction companies also to a "cheap deal",[2] and the purchase of an already discounted firm as Angwin (2007) suggested might entail capital gains for the bidder.

2 The expression "cheap deal" refers to targets of M&A transactions, which might be undervalued (Wernerfelt, 1984).

Table 2.7: CAAR of Financial Investments and Financial Difficulties

Investment Purchase by Financial Firms ; N=15				
Event Window	[-20,+20]	[-10,+10]	[-5;+5]	[-1,+1]
CAAR	8.31%	0.85%	0.62%	2.85%
Median	2.50%	0.13%	1.93%	4.04%
Min-Value	-16.56%	-18.72%	-18.15%	-11.34%
Max-Value	67.66%	33.93%	17.41%	22.88%
Positive	53.33%	53.33%	53.33%	60.00%
Financial Instability of Construction Firm; N=8				
Event Window	[-20,+20]	[-10,+10]	[-5,+5]	[-1,+1]
CAAR	0.81%	3.89%	1.67%	1.01%
Median	0.18%	3.56%	0.68%	0.49%
Min-Value	-16.56%	-14.44%	-14.16%	-5.95%
Max-Value	13.99%	19.15%	12.79%	9.22%
Positive	50.00%	75.00%	62.50%	50.00%
Difference Test				
Mean: t-value	0.798	-0.514	-0.269	0.618
Median: z-score	0.000	0.871	0.290	-0.419

Table 2.7 illustrates the average and medians of the cumulated abnormal returns of 23 takeovers by non-construction firms worldwide that either purchased a constructions firm to make a financial investment or due to financial problems of the construction firm in the period from 1985 until 2004. *, **, *** indicate the statistical significance to the 10%, 5% and 1% level, respectively, applying the Boehmer test at the CAAR values and the Wilcoxon-Signed-Rank test at the median values. The Min-Value refers to the company with the lowest abnormal returns resulting from the takeover. The Max-Value refers to the company with the highest abnormal returns resulting from the takeover. The Positive-Value refers to the percentage of takeovers with positive abnormal returns.

2.4.3 Domestic and International Takeovers

The globalization of the business activities also affects broadly the strategic behavior of construction firms. Several foreign markets offer lucrative construction projects due to their strong economic growth, such as the Chinese economy during the last decade. The volume of construction works and services in China rose by 19%–26% in the period of 2000–2005. A driving aspect of this development was related to the general surge of construction activities due to the Olympic Games in 2008, but this rate is not supposed to drop deeply, as the Chinese government plans to invest circa one trillion USD on infrastructure projects during the next 10 years (National Bureau of Statistics China, 2008). On the other hand, in some other markets, the demand for construction work grew only slowly or even declined over the last years. This accounts, for example, for the European market, in particular for the Western part. Nevertheless, the market volume of the European market amounts to 1,065bn USD and belongs to the biggest construction markets worldwide (Euroconstruct, 2007). Hence, entering and competing on this market may be still highly attractive for construction firms. Common strategies to enter a new market are either the foundation of foreign agencies or the acquisition of an already operating competitor abroad. The second option usually provides the advantage to get access to resources essential for the competition and the organizational survival on the foreign market (Conklin, 2005).

The internationalization of the business also fosters the development of management and other firm-specific skills, as many country-specific competencies are insufficiently exchangeable between countries (Nocke and Yeaple, 2007). On the other hand, firms transfer their knowledge and capabilities such as superior technology or marketing skills to the acquired foreign firm, thereby trying to enhance the market share and even to prevent potential competitors from the market entry (Morck and Yeung, 1991). As with horizontal takeovers, companies can exploit synergies and enlarge the company size and their global market power through related international M&A (Seth et al., 2002). Particularly, the increased international firm's size is of significant relevance for construction companies, because the bigger a construction firm the higher its reputation to be able to handle huge international construction projects (see also chapter 2.1). Further reasons include the opportunity to arbitrage the different tax regimes among countries, the reduction of the company's risk and the consequent cheaper financing costs, the declined bankruptcy probability as well as the improved ability to raise debt (Markides and Ittner, 1994). Not surprisingly, Corhay (2000) reports on his investigated sample the positive wealth effects for bidders of international M&A.

Despite these numerous benefits from international diversification, there is also evidence that the costs of international diversification and managerial hubris can surpass the potential benefits. Denis et al. (2002) provide a reference for this argument by illustrating the negative impact on shareholder wealth, which is comparable to the discounts of industrial diversification. Eckbo and Thorburn (2000) do not show these strong negative wealth effects of international acquisitions but only report a general superiority of domestic to international takeovers. The results for the construction industry comply mainly with these latter findings:

Both groups achieve positive CAAR values at all event windows, but the domestic takeovers outperform the international ones by 1.33%, 1.56% and 0.76% at the 11, 21 and 41-day observation period, though the reliability for the international sample is constrained due to a missing significance of the results. Only at the shortest event window the international M&A are significant and achieve the same CAAR values as the domestic sample. Still the risk of losing tremendous money seems in domestic M&A (Min-Value of -66.56%) higher than in internationals (Min-value of -36.74%).

Table 2.8: CAAR of Domestic and International Takeovers

Domestic Takeovers; N=260				
Event Window	[-20,+20]	[-10,+10]	[-5;+5]	[-1,+1]
CAAR	2.56%***	2.84%***	1.63%***	1.1%***
Median	2.12%**	2.99%***	0.52%**	0.69%***
Min-Value	-66.56%	-35.48%	-25.25%	-17.36%
Max-Value	60.79%	59.95%	34.59%	27.83%
Positive	54.23%	59.23%	53.46%	57.31%
International Takeovers; N=94				
Event Window	[-20,+20]	[-10,+10]	[-5,+5]	[-1,+1]
CAAR	1.80%	1.28%	0.30%	1.1%**
Median	0.58%	0.36%	0.42%	0.81%**
Min-Value	-36.74%	-27.39%	-32.63%	-11.34%
Max-Value	67.66%	40.33%	27.80%	16.78%
Positive	51.58%	49.47%	50.53%	56.84%
Difference Test				
Mean: t-value	0.409	1.147	1.245	0.008
Median: z-score	-0.645	-1.081	-0.727	0.093

Table 2.8 illustrates the average and medians of the cumulated abnormal returns of 354 quoted firms worldwide that conducted a domestic or international takeover within the construction industry in the period from 1985 until 2004. *, **, *** indicate the statistical significance to the 10%, 5% and 1% level, respectively, applying the Boehmer test at the CAAR values and the Wilcoxon-Signed-Rank test at the median values. The Min-Value refers to the company with the lowest abnormal returns resulting from the takeover. The Max-Value refers to the company with the highest abnormal returns resulting from the takeover. The Positive-Value refers to the percentage of takeovers with positive abnormal returns.

An explanation for the dominance of the domestic takeovers might be the real estate boom in Ireland, Spain, the United Kingdom and the United States from the mid-nineties until 2007. To test the influence of the takeovers within these countries, I divide the domestic sample into acquisitions within these countries and countries not undergoing a real estate boom.

The results in table 2.9 imply that a major part of the positive CAAR on domestic takeovers consists of the bidder gains within Ireland, Spain, UK and the US. However, if these countries are excluded from the domestic sample, the positive CAAR values of domestic acquisition drop and nearly coincide with the abnormal returns of international acquisitions. Hence, the main part of the positive abnormal returns of domestic takeovers result from an exaggeration in the real estate market and not a sustainable advantage of domestic to international acquisitions.

Table 2.9: Detailed CAAR Analysis of Domestic Takeovers

Domestic Takeovers in E, IRL, UK, US; N=167				
Event Window	[-20,+20]	[-10,+10]	[-5;+5]	[-1,+1]
CAAR	3.13%**	3.31%***	1.73%**	0.71%*
Median	3.46%***	4.03%***	0.67%**	0.43%*
Min-Value	-65.56%	-35.48%	-25.25%	-17.36%
Max-Value	60.79%	37.93%	26.97%	13.60%
Positive	57.49%	62.28%	53.89%	54.49%
Domestic Takeovers excluding E, IRL, UK, US; N=93				
Event Window	[-20,+20]	[-10,+10]	[-5,+5]	[-1,+1]
CAAR	1.56%	2.01%	1.46%	1.79%**
Median	-0.65%	0.87%	0.36%	0.80%
Min-Value	31.22%	10.79%	14.44%	1.41%
Max-Value	75.48%	30.00%	44.01%	1.65%
Positive	48.39%	53.76%	52.69%	62.37%
Difference Test				
Mean: t-value	0.814	0.912	0.299	1.290
Median: z-score	1.574	1.685*	0.844	0.694

Table 2.9 illustrates the average and medians of the cumulated abnormal returns of 167 quoted firms from Ireland, Spain, UK and US and 93 quoted firms from any country excluding the previous four that conducted a domestic takeover within the construction industry in the period from 1985 until 2004. *, **, *** indicate the statistical significance to the 10%, 5% and 1% level, respectively, applying the Boehmer test at the CAAR values and the Wilcoxon-Signed-Rank test at the median values. The Min-Value refers to the company with the lowest abnormal returns resulting from the takeover. The Max-Value refers to the company with the highest abnormal returns resulting from the takeover. The Positive-Value refers to the percentage of takeovers with positive abnormal returns.

When comparing domestic and international takeovers for construction bidders, the CAAR values diverge to a percentage of 3.22% at the 41-day event period. Domestic takeovers entail on all event windows positive excess value, but international acquisitions depict mainly negative effects. Still the risk of losing tremendous money seems in domestic M&A (Min-Value of -51.40%) higher than in internationals (Min-value of -36.74%). Nevertheless, this sample is also biased by the domestic takeovers in Ireland, Spain, UK and the US likewise to the overall sample, which constrains the interpretation of the results.

Table 2.10: CAAR of Domestic and International Takeovers by Construction Firms

Domestic Takeovers; N=188				
Event Window	[-20,+20]	[-10,+10]	[-5;+5]	[-1,+1]
CAAR	2.63%**	2.80%***	1.54%**	0.82%**
Median	2.50**%	3.20%***	0.37%*	0.60%**
Min-Value	-51.40%	-25.43%	-21.50%	-16.80%
Max-Value	60.79%	37.93%	34.04%	18.96%
Positive	55.85%	59.04%	52.66%	57.45%
International Takeovers; N=55				
Event Window	[-20,+20]	[-10,+10]	[-5,+5]	[-1,+1]
CAAR	-0.59%	-0.24%	-0.48%	1.19%
Median	-1.11%	-0.54%	0.02%	0.66%
Min-Value	-36.74%	-27.39%	-32.63%	-9.64%
Max-Value	29.99%	17.78%	20.56%	16.78%
Positive	45.45%	45.45%	49.09%	58.18%
Difference Test				
Mean: t-value	1.397	1.861*	1.533	-0.449
Median: z-score	-1.415	-1.557	-0.722	0.332

Table 2.10 illustrates the average and medians of the cumulated abnormal returns of 243 quoted construction firms worldwide that conducted a domestic or international takeover in the period from 1985 until 2004. *, **, *** indicate the statistical significance to the 10%, 5% and 1% level, respectively, applying the Boehmer test at the CAAR values and the Wilcoxon-Signed-Rank test at the median values. The Min-Value refers to the company with the lowest abnormal returns resulting from the takeover. The Max-Value refers to the company with the highest abnormal returns resulting from the takeover. The Positive-Value refers to the percentage of takeovers with positive abnormal returns.

The picture for non-construction firms is twofold. Both samples exclusively show positive abnormal returns, but domestic takeovers out pass the international acquisitions on the smaller two event windows. However, on the 21- and 41-day event windows the international takeovers outstrip by 0.41% and 2.72% respectively the national counterparts. It seems as if the non-construction firms prepare and conduct their international acquisition activities more thoroughly than construction enterprises. At least the capital market expects non-construction firms to exploit value-increasing potentials by international diversification into the construction industry. Although the domestic acquisitions are positively influenced by the aforementioned takeovers within four specific countries, the capital market positively acknowledges the international engagement of non-construction firms as can be seen on the significant 5.10% excess value at the [-20;20] event window. The 61.54% takeovers with positive results stress this finding.

Table 2.11: CAAR of Domestic and International Takeovers by Non-Construction Firms

Domestic Takeovers; N=72				
Event Window	[-20,+20]	[-10,+10]	[-5;+5]	[-1,+1]
CAAR	2.38%	2.97%*	1.88%	1.83%*
Median	0.15%	1.76%*	1.20%	0.78%*
Min-Value	-66.56%	-35.48%	-25.25%	-17.36%
Max-Value	50.38%	59.95%	34.59%	27.83%
Positive	50.00%	59.72%	55.56%	56.94%
International Takeovers; N=39				
Event Window	[-20,+20]	[-10,+10]	[-5,+5]	[-1,+1]
CAAR	5.10%*	3.38%	1.37%	0.97%
Median	2.24%	3.02%	1.14%	0.83%
Min-Value	-21.17%	-20.91%	-18.15%	-11.34%
Max-Value	67.56%	40.33%	27.80%	15.26%
Positive	61.54%	56.41%	53.85%	56.41%
Difference Test				
Mean: t-value	0.798	0.160	-0.264	-0.675
Median: z-score	0.658	0.133	-0.374	-0.287

Table 2.11 illustrates the average and medians of the cumulated abnormal returns of 111 quoted non-constrcuction firms worldwide that purchased a construction firm domestically or internationally in the period from 1985 until 2004. *, **, *** indicate the statistical significance to the 10%, 5% and 1% level, respectively, applying the Boehmer test at the CAAR values and the Wilcoxon-Signed-Rank test at the median values. The Min-Value refers to the company with the lowest abnormal returns resulting from the takeover. The Max-Value refers to the company with the highest abnormal returns resulting from the takeover. The Positive-Value refers to the percentage of takeovers with positive abnormal returns.

2.4.4 M&A Across Decades

Pauser et al. (2007) display a boost in firm value for construction bidders since 1993 due to M&A activity. For the first seven observed years, they show a negative impact. They trace the negative results to the critical assessment of the capital market about conglomerate and horizontal takeovers. The assumption is vague, as the number of six observed cases is even smaller than my panel size for the same period. In addition, I notice that this does not only account for these types of acquisitions but affects all takeovers within the construction industry. Likewise to the previous study these results are insignificant.

During the second period (1993–1999), the acquirer discounts switch to stable and significant positive CAAR, and in the most recent period (2000–2004), the excess value of bidder companies even further rises to values of 3.35%. Thus the capital market most probably honors the consolidation process within the construction industry. These findings are partially in line with Pauser et al.

(2007), who report positive CAAR values for both periods as well, which, however, slightly decrease from the second to the third time period.

Table 2.12: CAAR at Different Time Periods

Time Period a: 1985-1992; N=21				
Event Window	[-20,+20]	[-10,+10]	[-5;+5]	[-1,+1]
CAAR	-3.40%	-0.38%	-0.78%	-0.28%
Median	-3.24%	-3.37%	-3.36%	-0.68%
Min-Value	-12.85%	-9.29%	-12.82%	-7.28%
Max-Value	7.66%	11.94%	10.31%	5.67%
Positive	33.33%	44.44%	44.44%	33.33%
Time Period b: 1993-1999; N=134				
Event Window	[-20,+20]	[-10,+10]	[-5;+5]	[-1,+1]
CAAR	1.63%	1.34%	1.37%*	1.17%**
Median	2.05%	0.13%	0.20%	0.53%**
Min-Value	-66.56%	-35.48%	-25.25%	-17.36%
Max-Value	55.20%	40.33%	34.04%	22.88%
Positive	54.48%	50.34%	51.72%	57.24%
Time Period c: 2000-2004; N=199				
Event Window	[-20,+20]	[-10,+10]	[-5;+5]	[-1,+1]
CAAR	3.16%***	3.35%***	1.30%**	1.11%***
Median	2.12%**	3.38%***	0.98%*	0.76%***
Min-Value	-36.74%	-25.43%	-32.63%	-16.19%
Max-Value	67.66%	59.95%	34.59%	27.83%
Positive	54.55%	62.63%	54.55%	59.09%
Difference Test; Time Period a - b				
Mean: t-value	-1.010	0.435	0.712	0.736
Median: z-score	-1.465	-0.631	-0.853	-0.838
Difference Test; Time Period a - c				
Mean: t-value	-1.184	-0.973	-0.681	-0.733
Median: z-score	-1.365	-1.127	-0.770	-0.776
Difference Test; Time Period b - c				
Mean: t-value	-0.883	-1.619	0.071	0.090
Median: z-score	-0.442	-2.008	-0.177**	0.069

Table 2.12 illustrates the average and medians of the cumulated abnormal returns of 354 quoted firms worldwide that conducted a takeover within the construction industry in the different time period of 1985-1992, 1993-1999 and 2000-2004. *, **, *** indicate the statistical significance to the 10%, 5% and 1% level, respectively, applying the Boehmer test at the CAAR values and the Wilcoxon-Signed-Rank test at the median values. The Min-Value refers to the company with the lowest abnormal returns resulting from the takeover. The Max-Value refers to the company with the highest abnormal returns resulting from the takeover. The Positive-Value refers to the percentage of takeovers with positive abnormal returns.

2.5 Success Parameters of Takeovers

The following chapter analyzes the combined impact of potential factors on the success of a takeover by means of a multiple regression. The model is constituted to control for acquirer performance, leverage and risk, as well as transaction characteristics and macroeconomic influences:

i) Firm Specifics of Acquirer

1. Earnings per Share (EPS-ratio): Morck et al. (1990) state a positive impact of the acquiring firm performance on their wealth creation at takeovers. Put differently, managers of well-performing companies run the company in favor of the shareholder interest and use the resources for profitable projects.

2. Market to Book Ratio (M/B-ratio): The M/B-ratio is a valuation indicator for the company. Although historical performance is not necessarily a reliable indicator for future performance (Antoniou et al., 2007), a high M/B-ratio usually indicates positive expectations by the capital market for the future performance of the company (Rau and Vermaelen, 1998). I test for the impact of this indicator on the success of the transactions within the construction industry.

3. Leverage: A company's leverage may affect the returns associated with takeover announcements. Bruner (1988) describes bidders as low levered previous to successful transactions, which lever up during the next two years after merger.

ii) Transaction Characteristics

4. Strategic Focus: After analyzing the wealth effect of the various strategic takeover types for construction and non-construction firms, the effect of these types on the success of acquisition is tested.

5. Domestic vs. International: It is investigated whether the positive effects of domestic takeover – in particular within Ireland, Spain, UK and the US – also hold as explanatory variable at the regression analysis. In addition, the regression model tests for the influence of international takeovers on the accomplished abnormal returns of the bidders.

6. Private vs. Public Targets: Regarding Fuller et al. (2002), bidders gain form the acquisition of private targets but lose on acquisitions of publicly listed firms. This assumption complies with the presented value discounts of 15%–30% for private firms in comparison to similar public counterparts (Officer, 2007).

7. Hostile vs. Friendly Takeovers: If the transaction attitude is hostile, bidders usually have to pay a higher premium for the target than with friendly takeovers. This causes diminishing abnormal returns for the bidders (Goergen and Renneboog, 2004).

8. Method of Payment: Travlos (1987) demonstrates a relevant impact of the method of payment on the acquirer shareholder wealth at takeover announcements. Stock-financed takeovers induce bad news for the shareholders, as managers use stock as payment measure when they assume an overvaluation of their company. If the acquisition is cash financed, it implies good news. In this case managers suppose an undervaluation of their stocks and would rather use cash to avoid an overpayment for the target.

iii) Macroeconomic Aspects

9. Stock Market Bubble: With this variable I investigate the effect of the overall hype at the stock markets within the years 1999–2000 on the transactions in which construction companies were involved.

10. GDP and Real Estate Cycles: Further, I consider the relevance of GDP and real estate cycles for transactions. It is tested whether the GDP growth rates of the bidders' home countries have a relevant impact on the wealth effects of the M&A. The testing for GDP growth rates also is composed of real estate cycles since these are usually closely related to the respective macroeconomic developments of a country (Case et al., 2000; Rottke and Wernecke, 2002).

The regression analysis (see page 33) reveals the following variables as significant success parameters at takeovers within the construction industry: EPS, M/B-ratio, conglomerate diversification of construction firms and acquisition during exaggeration on the stock market (stock market bubble). If a company with convincing earnings per share or market to book ratio heads into a takeover, the capital market does not assess this engagement positively, but instead imposes a discount on the company value. Thus, in contrast to general expectations, the capital market believes that the company generates higher returns on a stand-alone basis than by enlarging the business.

The strategic focus does not display any impact on the abnormal returns, apart from the conglomerate diversifications of construction firms. Regarding the regression results and in line with the results from the analysis in chapter 2.4 conglomerate diversifications tend to entail a discount on the valuation of construction companies.

Finally, the stock market bubble causes an overvaluation of firms and also leads to exaggeration in the valuation of bidders involved in construction takeovers. Therefore, it can be assumed that a certain amount of the presented positive CAAR values for the periods 1993–1999 and 2000–2004 refers to the general overvaluation of firms during the stock market bubble at the end of the last millennium.

Table 2.13: Short-Term Regression Results

Explanatory Variables	M1	M2	M3	M4	M5	M6	M7
Constant	0.006 (0.415)	-0.001 (0.336)	0.022 (0.794)	0.065*** (-0.4452)	0.051*** (2.700)	0.001 (0.096)	-0.012 (-0.364)
Leverage		0.000 (-0.462)					
EPS-ratio	-0.004* (-1.718)			-0.002*** (2.614)		-0.002*** (-2.687)	
M/B-ratio	-0.005* (-1.732)				-0.004* (-1.783)		-0.005** (-2.094)
MV		0.000 (0.336)					
Domestic				-0.049 (-0.662)	-0.041 (-1.037)		
Domestic IRL,E,UK,US		0.014 (0.755)					0.018 (0.933)
International	0.037 (1.112)					0.044 (1.411)	0.044 (1.180)
Friendly		0.026 (0.921)					
Hostile				-0.005 (-0.225)			
Cash Financed		-0.005 (-0.276)					
Stock Financed				0.004 (0.194)			
Cash/Stock Financed			-0.008 (-0.299)				
Private		-0.017 (-0.828)					
Public	0.025 (1.361)						
Horizontal (Constr.)			0.003 (0.162)				
Vertical (Constr.)			-0.007 (-0.031)				
Conglomerate (Constr.)	-0.091*** (-3.443)				-0.083*** (-2.921)		-0.082*** (-2.966)
Vertical (Non-Constr.)				-0.002 (-0.092)			
Conglomerate (Non-Constr.)		0.073* (1.826)			0.035 (0.816)	0.042 (1.117)	
Financial Investment	0.133 (1.464)						
Financial Instability			-0.019 (-0.544)				
GDP			0.001 (0.266)				
Stock Market Bubble	0.047** (2.139)				0.058*** (2.600)	0.042** (2.091)	0.059*** (2.703)
Durbin-Watson	1.918	1.844	1.862	1.905	1.985	1.916	1.996
Adj. R^Square	0.082	0.009	0.002	0.007	0.057	0.033	0.076
N Obs	261	300	334	322	284	322	284

Table 2.13 illustrates the results of the multivariate linear regression model for the [-20;20] event window. *, **, *** indicate the statistical significance to the 10%, 5% and 1% level, respectively. The number in brackets presents the t-statistics. All test statistics are computed applying White's (1980) heteroskedasticity-consistent covariance matrix.

2.6 Conclusion

The initial objective of this research was to assess whether M&A transactions within the construction industry are an effective tool for a company to improve its difficult economic situation and create shareholder value. The study analyzes the shareholder value effects of M&A announcements on 354 bidder firms. The overall sample observes exclusively positive CAAR for bidder firms with a range of 1.09% to 2.34%. It can subsequently be stated that M&A announcements within the construction industry have positive value effects for bidding firms. This corresponds to the prior findings of Choi and Russel (2004), Delaney and Wamuziri (2004) as well as Pauser et al. (2007).

When the 354 takeovers are subdivided according to their strategic focuses, detailed implications emerge about the benefits and drawbacks of the particular business enlargement. Shareholders of bidding firms that are involved in horizontal takeovers gain significantly from the announcement (up to 2.88%). High expected synergies and the benefits from a bigger firm size imply these substantial value enhancements. Likewise, bidding firms extending their value chain also benefit from takeovers with a maximum CAAR of 3.34%. In particular the extension to downstream real estate services allows construction firms to generate more consistent revenues, which are then positively rewarded by the capital market. For conglomerate takeovers by construction firms, the picture shows negative wealth effects for shareholders. This is consistent with the recent research on conglomerate diversification, which reports no significant value effects or even value destruction as a result of business diversification.

Most surprisingly appear the highly positive effects for non-construction companies acquiring construction firms, especially when undergoing conglomerate acquisitions (up to 7.28% CAAR). The high gains on conglomerate acquisitions oppose the negative results of conglomerate acquisitions by construction firms. It seems as if the acquired construction companies increase the flexibility of strategic construction decisions and promise a positive contribution to the non-construction firm profits.

The picture for domestic versus international takeovers is inconsistent between construction firms and non-construction firms. In accordance to Denis et. al. (2002) and Mentz and Schiereck (2008) domestic acquisitions benefit construction firms and international acquisitions indicate no or a destructive wealth effect. Even though the high abnormal gains of domestic acquisitions partly results from national acquisitions in countries with a real estate boom, domestic takeovers can overall be accounted as the superior strategy for construction firms. Non-construction firms exploit strong positive wealth effects from domestic and international takeovers, whereas most results are insignificant. Hence, no clear picture can be drawn concerning a superior geographical acquisition strategy.

At regression analysis conglomerate diversifications of construction firms affect negatively bidder abnormal returns. This finding supports the results from the subsample analysis, that conglomerate diversification destroys shareholder value and should be avoided by construction companies. Of major interest is the final result: If a construction company is already successful and achieves a high EPS or MTBV, transactions are negatively rewarded. Thus, the capital market does not expect positive effects for the companies' earnings, but instead fears for a decline in earnings and economic devaluation from the takeover.

3 Strategic Bidders and Long-Run M&A Success Beyond Monopolistic Power

Abstract

The M&A success of strategic consolidation in various industries can be at least partly explained by increased market power, some potential for collusion or monopolistic price-setting capabilities. This is not the case within the construction industry. This industry is characterized by high fragmentation, very low market shares of even the largest corporations and hardly any potential for gaining significant market power through acquisitions. Nevertheless, the construction industry shows intensive M&A activity, and the question arises whether these transactions are favorable for the shareholders of the bidding companies.

The examination documents a remarkably positive long-run stock price performance for acquirers within the construction industry. The evidence not only accounts for strategic bidders, but also for construction firms diversifying their business by conglomerate acquisitions. The success is mainly driven by the transaction characteristics of profitability, capital structure, payment media and the kind of takeover.

3.1 Introduction

There has been plenty of research about the stock returns of bidding firms announcing M&A transactions. Most short-run event studies report either significant negative or sometimes insignificant abnormal returns for the acquirers around the takeover announcements (Andrade et al., 2001; Bruner, 2002; Campa and Hernando, 2006; Swanstrom, 2006). Subsequent to these short-term examinations, some studies extend the observation period to a long-run horizon. While Loughran and Vijh (1997) document positive wealth effects for the subsample of cash bidders on a five-year horizon, they also show, on average, a negative long-term performance for all bidders (cash and stock). Likewise, Agrawal and Samwick (2003), as well as Rau and Vermaelen (1998), illustrate negative wealth effects for acquirers within the five years after an acquisition.

These general findings do not distinguish between the abnormal stock returns for each industry, but report results for cross-industry observations. Consequently, the cross-industrial samples neglect industry-specific wealth effects. Additionally, the heterogeneous abnormal returns of the various industries often cause inconsistent results for the bidders (Stulz et al., 1990; Goergen and Renneborg, 2004; Gregory and McCorriston, 2005). Put differently, industries with specific production processes like the construction industry might show a distinct picture of wealth effects. Although the construction industry accounts for 10% of global GDP, it differs significantly in its operations and characteristics from other industries, suggesting different wealth effects at M&A transactions (McGraw-Hill Construction, 2007).

The size of a construction firm often determines the success at tendering for a new construction project. Projects principals recognize the firm size as the ability of the company to realize large construction projects (Delaney and Wamuziri, 2004). Particularly in large-scale technologically challenging projects, which are especially common in the civil engineering sector, size and financial strength define an essential prerequisite in customers' perception for conducting such projects successfully. Construction firms have to incur costly capital expenditures to utilize complex customized and high-tech machines such as huge drillers for tunnel construction (Gonzales et al., 1998). Hence, M&A might help the company to receive the required size, knowledge and capabilities to accomplish prestigious and often lucrative large-scale projects.

Unlike most manufacturing firms, construction companies do not produce a homogeneous mass, but unique customized products. Each new product needs new designs, plans, structures, operations and calculations (Welling and Kamann, 2001). The project uniqueness raises forecast uncertainty and the risk of unforeseen events as, for example, unpredicted soil conditions on the construction site that might negatively affect the project's financial result (Miozzo, 2002). Furthermore, an exact price calculation of the final product is difficult prior to completion due to the customization of each project and the customer's influence during the realization process (Egan, 1998). Likewise, working processes on the construction site vary widely between construction projects due to the nature of the different tasks and the involvement of several subcontractors. Especially the supervision of heterogeneous and constantly changing teams with different educational backgrounds may cause crucial problems to the success of the project (Kamann et al., 2006). Therefore, financial strength and sufficient corporate size is wanted to bear the risk of a financial failure of a project. According to Amihud et al. (1986), takeovers contribute to these requirements and reduce the risk of financial instability.

In addition to these production specifics, the construction market structure is characterized by high fragmentation, and construction firms face strong price competition when bidding for new projects. It is common practice that the project principal, especially public authorities, choose the contractor based on the lowest offered price for the project (Ball, 1996). Construction firms must calculate their construction costs tightly and are forced to find appropriate subcontractors for the various lots of a construction project, which they do not produce themselves. The conventional procedure to select an adequate subcontractor is calling for a tender for several lots (Latham, 1994). Nevertheless, this procedure often entails an adversarial relationship between the general contractor and the subcontractor. Because the contract is supposed to last for only that one project, every party tries to extract the maximum profit from the temporary alliance. Thus, a construction firm faces the risk of moral hazard with opportunistic behavior of subcontractors. It is a common occurrence that subcontractors deliver lower than requested quality when they are in a short-term contract with a general contractor (Haksever et al., 2001). In the worst case, a subcontractor fails during the project. Such incidents can entail delays in the construction process and consequently cause huge penalty payments for the general contractor. Due to these drawbacks, conventional subcontractor selection often leads to higher–than-expected costs of a construction project (Egan, 1998). At the same time, a rising number of customers demand more stringent quality assurance from construction firms (Barlow and Jashapara, 1998). Customers increasingly request a well guarantee for structured and organized supply chain, in order to receive a higher reliability and quality of the construction services (Briscoe et al., 2001). To avoid opportunistic subcontractor behavior and the subsequent financial risks as well as to raise the profitability and the chance to acquire new projects, construction firms in recent years show a tendency to more often partnering relationships with their subcontractors (Phua, 2006).

Partnering in the construction industry refers to a close cooperation between two parties. The cooperation is characterized by shared targets, aligned working processes and mutual-benefit seeking, as well as respect and trust between the two parties (Lu and Yan, 2007). The common forms of partnering between two construction firms or a construction firm and a subcontractor are project or strategic partnerships. Project partnering is often used by general contractors to bid on a team for a project and to share the operational as well as financial risk of large-scale projects (Black et al., 2000). This form of partnering also provides the opportunity to test a partnership before extending it to a strategic one (Li et al., 2001). Strategic partnerships are usually long-term relationships and play an important role in the construction industry, because of the high-value experience transfer between the projects (Beach et al., 2005).

Partnering also permits to shift contractual relationships toward a collaborative team-work model, thereby avoiding adversarial behavior between the involved parties. Partnering motivates firms to jointly and efficiently plan working processes on construction sites. Better coordination of actions permits firms to employ their resources more effectively and consequently to raise their productivity (New and Ramsey, 1997). Collaboration also increases the potential to fulfill the product quality demands of the customers adequately. Haksever et al. (2001) report a 20% rise in the quality of construction projects because of cooperation during the design and planning of a project. Likewise, Scott (2001) reports a remarkable increase in the precise cost and time forecasts of the projects, and Beach et al. (2005) document a significant cost decrease owing to the reduction of litigations with subcontractors. In addition to these findings, Black et al. (2000) see partnerships as a proven means for entering new markets and setting up businesses abroad. Through an international partner, the foreign general contractor gains worthwhile knowledge about the cultural and legal issues of the host country.

Although partnerships, in particular those with a long-term strategic focus, allow a close cooperation to exist between construction firms, a partnership is still a loose network. Construction firms face the threat that an essential partner might drop out of the partnership and take all the obtained knowledge with it. This risk and the general distrust that partners might abuse partnerships to cause damage to the counterpart can restrain construction firms from seeking long-term partnerships (Bresnen and Marshall, 2000). Alternatively, construction companies can integrate the subcontractor or a competitor in order to incorporate strategically important knowledge and to achieve the aforementioned long-term benefits. In recent years, more construction firms enlarge their value chain to up- or downstream-related businesses like project development or facility management in order to increase the efficiency of their value chain and subsequently their productivity and performance (Claessens et al., 2003; Fan and Goyal, 2006). Others seek a strategic corporate advantage by purchasing companies from other business sectors (Martin and Sayrak, 2003). Several non-construction firms also intend to profit from the long-term cooperation benefits within the construction industry by acquiring construction firm units. While the intensifying of partnering is one industry-specific reason for M&A, other arguments in favour of the acquisition of construction firms also show business-related characteristics. The vertical extension of up- or downstream related companies toward the actual construction business is one common acquisition strategy. Firms not directly related to the construction industry acquire construction firms in order to decrease their dependence on purchasing construction services for future projects in the market. Finally, some project principals purchase construction firms, as they fear bankruptcy and failure of the construction firm or at least costly interruptions In this case, M&A transactions are supposed to guarantee the continuation of the project (Thomson Financial, 2008). Financial difficulties can also be the reason for an acquisition by financial institutions, as those expect fewer losses from the acquisition than the failure of the construction firm. Real estate investment trusts (REITs) and private equity funds tend to use the acquisitions as a long-term investment with the target realizing abundant efficiency potentials at construction firms (Thomson Financial, 2008).

Indeed, there is a good amount of research about strategic partnering within the construction industry, but to the best of my knowledge it has not been analyzed thus far, whether M&A within the construction industry create value for the bidding firms in the long run. Although the distinct characteristics of the construction industry, as well as the contract design of partnering, suggest benefits from long-term strategic cooperation, there is no evidence on the long-term effects of M&A on shareholder value in the construction industry. Several short-term event studies about the wealth effects for bidders at M&A announcements promote this hypothesis. For instance, studies on domestic takeovers within the construction industry by Choi and Russel (2004) and Delaney and Wamuziri (2004), who also include the construction material industry, indicate positive share price reactions for the bidding companies. Pauser et al. (2007) extend the focus and investigate takeovers within the construction industry on a global scale. They report, on average, positive abnormal returns for the target and the combined entity and slightly positive results for the acquirer. In another global short-term event study with a broader sample, Rottke et al. (2009) document clear positive short-term abnormal returns for the bidders at takeovers within the construction industry.

In this study, I illustrate the wealth effects of M&A within the construction industry in the long run by examining a long-term capital market analysis. Although long-term cross-industry studies generally report negative wealth effects for acquiring firms, the partnering research documents positive effects for construction firms in long-term collaborations. Subsequently, M&A within the construction industry are supposed to generate different long-term wealth effects as suggested by cross-industry studies. Next to a general overview about the long-term value effects of M&A within the construction industry, I investigate the wealth effects of the various strategic focuses of the takeovers. Since I concentrate on a global scale, I also differentiate between the wealth effects of national vs. cross-border takeovers.

The study is organized as follows. Section 3.2 introduces the applied data set and methodology. The long-term capital market reactions at M&A in the construction industry are highlighted in section 3.3. A detailed regression analysis on long-term returns illustrates the potential success factors of the takeovers in section 3.4. Section 3.5 concludes by summarizing the main findings and implications.

3.2 Data and Methodology

3.2.1 Data

I select the M&A events with participation of construction firms from the Thomson One Database (Thomson Financial, 2008). As I focus on the long-term bidder returns of construction firms engaging in a takeover or a non-construction company purchasing a construction firm, I choose all M&A transactions that reference construction firms either as a bidder or as a target. I apply the SIC for the classification of the construction (1500 – 1799) and non-construction firms.

Table 3.1: Sample Overview of Construction Firms as Bidders

Year	N	Horizontal	Vertical	Conglomerate	Domestic	Cross Border	Total Transaction Volume (mn USD)	Avergage Transaction Volume (mn USD)
2004	13	4	7	2	13	0	1,180.49	90.81
2003	24	16	6	2	17	7	6,043.10	251.80
2002	36	25	8	3	30	6	6,209.15	172.48
2001	29	18	6	5	23	6	7,600.31	262.08
2000	42	23	8	11	27	15	8,319.62	198.09
1999	27	11	7	9	16	11	10,475.37	387.98
1998	27	15	10	2	25	2	3,832.04	141.93
1997	9	7	1	1	7	2	1,536.51	170.72
1996	12	4	7	1	9	3	1,089.87	90.82
1995	8	7	0	1	5	3	604.07	75.51
1994	5	2	3	0	5	0	346.98	69.40
1993	1	1	0	0	1	0	34.52	34.52
1992	3	3	0	0	3	0	128.99	43.00
1991	1	0	0	1	1	0	32.77	32.77
1990	2	1	1	0	2	0	52.67	26.34
1989	2	0	1	1	2	0	201.86	100.93
1988	1	0	1	0	1	0	31.94	31.94
1987	1	0	1	0	1	0	52.10	52.10
1986	0	0	0	0	0	0	0.00	0.00
1985	0	0	0	0	0	0	0.00	0.00
Σ	**243**	**137**	**67**	**39**	**188**	**55**	**47,772.35**	**2,233.19**

Table 3.1 illustrates the takeovers by construction firms in the period 1985–2004. The bidder sample is subdivided into its different strategic and geographical focuses. The total transaction volume refers to the cumulated transaction volume of all bidders within one year.

I include all deals in the period from 1982 to 2004. The minimum transaction value must amount to USD 20mn. Besides, the acquirer has to intend to own at least 50% + 1 share of the entire equity, thereby gaining control over the target. The acquiring company has to be listed on a public stock exchange during the time and up to a three-year observation period after the M&A announcement. On contrary, the target can either be a public or private company. By applying these criteria, I obtain 354 takeovers. 243 bidders are construction firms and 111 bidders are non-construction companies. Table 3.1 depicts in detail the takeovers initiated by construction companies regarding their year of occurrence, the strategic focus, the internationality and the transaction volume per year and table 3.2 illustrates the respective information of 111 bidders from outside of the construction industry.

Table 3.2: Sample Overview of Non-Construction Firms as Bidders

Year	N	Vertical	Conglom-erate	Financial Investment	Financial Difficulties	Domestic	Cross Border	Total Transaction Volume (mn USD)	Avergage Transaction Volume (mn USD)
2004	4	3	0	1	0	3	1	333.71	83.43
2003	9	6	0	3	0	7	2	2,150.50	238.94
2002	14	9	3	2	0	8	6	1,883.32	134.52
2001	13	8	5	0	0	7	6	809.78	62.29
2000	15	7	4	2	2	8	7	3,200.69	213.38
1999	13	8	2	2	1	11	2	1,578.42	121.42
1998	10	9	0	1	0	7	3	748.02	74.80
1997	3	2	1	0	0	3	0	2,798.60	932.87
1996	9	5	1	1	3	5	4	2,220.34	246.70
1995	5	4	0	1	0	3	2	592.36	118.47
1994	5	4	0	0	0	2	3	236.06	47.21
1993	0	0	0	0	0	0	0	0.00	0.00
1992	0	0	0	0	0	0	0	0.00	0.00
1991	2	2	0	0	0	2	0	3,287.97	1,643.98
1990	4	2	0	0	2	4	0	2,135.33	533.83
1989	2	1	0	1	0	1	1	1,318.40	659.20
1988	1	1	0	0	0	0	1	49.63	49.63
1987	1	0	0	1	0	1	0	30.12	30.12
1986	0	0	0	0	0	0	0	0.00	0.00
1985	1	0	1	0	0	0	1	445.00	445.00
Σ	**111**	**71**	**17**	**15**	**8**	**72**	**39**	**23,818.22**	**5,635.80**

Table 3.2 illustrates the takeovers of construction firms by non-construction firms in the period 1985–2004.The non-construction bidders is subdivided into the strategic focuses and backgrounds of the acquisitions. The total transaction volume refers to the cumulated transaction volume of all bidders within one year. The high average transaction volumes in the years 1989, 1990 and 1991 result from the small number of identified acquisition complying with the selection criteria. In addition, in 1991 the English conglomerate Hanson PLC bought Beazer PLC, one of the biggest residential constructors and producer of constructing aggregates in the US for nearly 3 bn USD (Thomson Financial, 2008; Austin, 1992).

The two tables show a steady increase of takeover activities within the construction industry, only interrupted by a small decline in 2003 and 2004 due to the effects of the recession after the bursting of the new economy bubble. Almost all strategic focuses at both groups undergo remarkable growth rates. Even though there is a trend to operate more internationally, domestic takeovers still account for the majority of the acquisitions within the construction industry.

3.2.2 Methodology

In contrast to short-term analyses, long-term performance investigation faces several methodological difficulties that can severely bias the calculated results (Barber and Lyon, 1997; Kothari and Warner, 1997). For analyzing the stock price performance, I compare the samples with reference portfolios considering the following potential biases of the reference portfolios: Reference portfolios may be composed of newly listed firms, which are added to the stock market index subsequent to the event month (new listing bias). The examined sample is not rebalanced during its observation time, but the returns of the reference portfolios or market indices are usually rebalanced periodically. When shares are rebalanced, commonly shares with positive returns are replaced against shares with negative returns (rebalancing bias). In addition, long-run abnormal returns are often positively skewed and require particular testing procedures (skewness bias). Knowing about these biases, I adjust the selected benchmark portfolios and apply adequate test statistics in order to avoid any result distortion.

There are two conventional methodologies for measuring long-term stock performance after a corporate event. Fama (1998) and Mitchell and Stafford (2000) propose the calendar-time methodology to evaluate the long-term performance of M&A events. The main advantage of this procedure is the avoidance of cross-sectional correlation of M&A events. However, in my analysis, only one sector, the construction industry, is analyzed. The calendar time methodology also avoids a cross-dependency of abnormal returns. As a result, the abnormal returns are not skewed, and standard statistical tests are sufficient to test the robustness of the achieved results. However, the skewness of abnormal returns can also be considered with skewness-adjusted t-test and bootstrapped t-statistics. On the other hand, Loughran and Ritter (2000) ascertain an underestimation of abnormal returns due to the equally weighted monthly abnormal returns and the weak representative benchmarks at the calendar time methodology. As well as this, the coefficients of the usually applied three- (Fama and French, 1993) or four-factor models (Carhart, 1997) can suffer from heteroskedasticity (Mitchell and Stafford, 2000).

With buy-and-hold abnormal return methodology (BHAR), these drawbacks can be avoided, and abnormal returns with a higher statistical power can be accomplished (Loughran and Ritter, 2000). With the BHAR approach, the stock returns of the firms experiencing a corporate event like a M&A announcement are compared to the stock performance of firms without such an event, but which display similar corporate characteristics as the sample firms. Common characteristics for selecting representative benchmark firms are the size and the market-to-book equity ratio (Barber and Lyon, 1997). If a firm has a comparable market capitalization or a market-to-book value in the range of 70% to 130% of an examined sample firm, it is accounted as a representative match and used for the reference portfolio for the respecting sample firm (Lyon et al., 1999). I also build reference portfolios by combining the market capitalization and the market-to-book value criteria.

Since I examine M&A events only within the construction industry, I exclusively select construction firms for the reference portfolios when analyzing the BHAR of construction firms. Likewise, I compare each non-construction bidder only with reference portfolios from its respecting industry. After detecting a reference portfolio for each bidder, I calculate the BHAR for each firm i for T months:

$$BHAR_{i,[t,T]} = \prod_{t=1}^{T}(1+R_{i,t}) - \prod_{t=1}^{T}(1+R_{j,t})$$

The cumulated product of the company's monthly returns $(1+R_{i,t})$ refers to the buy-and-hold return of firm i over the time interval from t to T. The cumulated product of the portfolio returns $(1+R_{j,t})$ represents the buy-and-hold return of the reference portfolio j for the same time interval as the examined sample. After calculating the BHAR for each firm, I determine the mean and median BHARs for all subgroups I focus on. The investigated period is 12, 24 and 36 months. According to Mitchell and Stafford (2000), time horizons longer than 36 months usually do not produce more reliable results for the determination of the long-term effects of M&A events. Besides, Cowan and Sergeant (2001) discovered that BHAR of up to 36 months suffer significantly less from distortions than BHAR of longer time periods.

For the robustness evaluation of the achieved results I apply several test statistics. First, I test whether the mean of the BHAR is different from zero with the conventional t-test. Since BHAR distributions may suffer from the aforementioned positive skewness, I also apply skewness-adjusted t-statistics as suggested by Lyon et al. (1999). In addition, I bootstrap the test statistic. As Sutton (1993) and Lyon et al. (1999) state, bootstrapping procedures deliver exact results for the skewness-adjusted test statistic. At the applied bootstrapping procedure, 1,000 bootstrapped resamples are withdrawn randomly from the original sample of size $n_b = n/2$ and for each resample the skewness adjusted t-statistic is calculated.[3] Through this procedure, I retrieve the t-statistic for each bootstrapped

3 Resamples with a size of n/2 yield more reliable test statistics with respect to the skewness adjustment than resample of size n (Bickel, Gotze and van Zwet, 1997; Shao, 1996).

sample, compare those with the t-statistic of the original sample and determine whether the received skewness adjusted t-statistic from the sample is significant. With the non-parametric Wilcoxon signed rank sum test, the robustness of the results is cross checked.

3.3 Empirical Results

In this chapter, I illustrate the long-term wealth effects from M&A activities within the construction industry. In the illustration process, I analyze the bidder BHAR from various dimensions. I begin with an illumination of the wealth effects for the overall construction and non-construction bidder sample. Afterward, I investigate the wealth effects for the various strategic focuses, and finally I discuss the results for the national and international acquisitions.

Since the combined (CB) reference portfolio only consists of rivals, which match the market value (MV) and market-to-book value (MTBV) criteria, it can be accounted for as the most precise reference portfolio. The mostly lower standard deviation of the results at the CB-portfolio approach in comparison to the MV and MTBV approach strengthen this statement. Hence, I refer in the analysis to the performance comparison of the sample to the CB-reference portfolio. The results from the MV and MTBV approach serve as a robustness check.

3.3.1 Overall Sample Analysis

Table 3.3 depicts the 12, 24 and 36 months BHAR for the overall construction and non-construction bidder samples yielded in comparison to the reference samples consisting of market value (MV), market-to-book value (MTBV) and combined (CB) portfolios.

The results show positive average abnormal returns of 23% for construction bidders in comparison to the rivals within the 36 months after a takeover event. However, the median results display with values of 0%–1% neutral effects from transactions. The divergence between mean and median returns coincides with the expectation of skewed results and indicates no specific performance implications for most construction firms but strong positive effects for few transactions. Despite these deviations, all results show a high significance.

The non-construction sample shows similar results. The average outperformance to competitors after a takeover of a construction firm amounts to BHAR values of 21%. The median values of non-construction firms exceed the performance of the reference samples only marginally. The performance to the other two reference portfolios stresses the illustrated results. According to the difference test, the means of construction and non-construction firms at least deviate significantly from each other at the MTBV approach.

Table 3.3: BHAR of Construction Firms and Non-Construction Firms

Construction Firms; N=243	Mean	t-value	p-value	Skewness Adjusted j-value	Skewness Adjusted p-value	Bootstrapped p-value	Median	Z-Score	P-value	Positives	Std. Dev.
One Year Event Period											
MV Portfolio	3.04%	1.878*	6.28%	1.932*	5.56%	4.50%**	-0.12%	-0.303	76.20%	44.72%	41.89%
MTBV Portfolio	12.22%	4.384***	0.00%	4.498***	0.00%	0.00%***	0.55%	-3.441***	0.06%	61.03%	32.52%
Combined Portfolio	22.18%	7.299***	0.00%	7.425***	0.00%	0.00%***	0.51%	-4.406***	0.00%	57.89%	17.96%
Two Years Event Period											
MV Portfolio	3.66%	2.064**	4.11%	2.130**	3.52%	3.10%**	0.17%	-0.512	60.84%	53.66%	42.93%
MTBV Portfolio	13.06%	4.518***	0.00%	4.640***	0.00%	0.00%***	0.88%	-5.218***	0.00%	66.18%	33.71%
Combined Portfolio	22.95%	7.369***	0.00%	7.499***	0.00%	0.00%***	0.89%	-5.222***	0.00%	66.32%	19.67%
Three Years Event Period											
MV Portfolio	3.41%	2.002**	4.75%	2.065**	4.10%	3.80%**	-0.11%	-0.199	84.20%	47.15%	42.46%
MTBV Portfolio	12.74%	4.485***	0.00%	4.605***	0.00%	0.00%***	0.59%	-5.024***	0.00%	64.71%	33.12%
Combined Portfolio	22.02%	7.045***	0.00%	7.474***	0.00%	0.00%***	0.73%	1.032***	0.00%	61.05%	18.88%
Non-Construction Firms; N=111											
One Year Event Period											
MV Portfolio	15.94%	3.002***	0.42%	3.137***	0.29%	0.10%***	0.87%	-2.990***	0.28%	63.27%	41.51%
MTBV Portfolio	25.59%	4.015***	0.02%	4.151***	0.01%	0.00%***	1.15%	-2.810***	0.50%	57.14%	44.61%
Combined Portfolio	21.56%	3.635***	0.07%	3.775***	0.04%	0.00%***	1.15%	-3.198***	0.14%	65.31%	37.17%
Two Years Event Period											
MV Portfolio	15.04%	2.828***	0.68%	2.948***	0.49%	0.30%***	0.14%	-1.746*	8.08%	63.27%	41.41%
MTBV Portfolio	24.73%	3.888***	0.03%	4.017***	0.02%	0.00%***	0.09%	-1.457	14.50%	55.10%	44.51%
Combined Portfolio	20.81%	3.517***	0.10%	3.649***	0.06%	0.00%***	0.36%	-2.481**	1.91%	63.27%	37.22%
Three Years Event Period											
MV Portfolio	14.43%	2.772***	0.79%	2.888***	0.58%	0.40%***	0.16%	-2.164**	3.05%	65.31%	41.29%
MTBV Portfolio	24.31%	3.839***	0.04%	3.964***	0.02%	0.00%***	0.22%	-1.558	11.95%	59.18%	44.33%
Combined Portfolio	20.51%	3.476***	0.11%	3.604***	0.07%	0.00%***	0.30%	-2.482**	1.31%	63.27%	36.44%
Difference Test	**1 Year:**			**2 Years:**			**3 Years:**				
Constr. Vs. Non-Constr.	**t-value**	**z-score**		**t-value**	**z-score**		**t-value**	**z-score**			
MV Portfolio	0.621	0.555		0.742	-0.077		0.743	0.198			
MTBV Portfolio	-2.275**	-0.061		-2.096**	-0.948		-2.167**	-1.109			
Combined Portfolio	-1.541	1.502		-1.373	0.552		-1.412	0.845			

Table 3.3 illustrates the average and medians of the buy-and-hold abnormal returns (BHAR) of 243 quoted construction firms as well as 111 quoted non-construction firms worldwide, which were involved in takeovers within the construction industry in the period from 1985 until 2004. As reference portfolios serve rivals with similar market values, market-to-book values and a combination of these two criteria. The significance for the average BHAR values is tested with the t-test, the skewness-adjusted t-test and the bootstrapping procedure. The median BHAR values are tested with the Wilcoxon-Signed-Rank test. *, **, *** indicate the statistical significance to the 10%, 5% and 1% level, respectively. The Positive-Value refers to the percentage of takeovers with positive abnormal returns. The standard deviation refers to the volatility of the BHAR.

Overall, M&A activities within the construction industry are worthwhile, regardless of whether the bidder is a construction firm or comes from another industry. On the one hand, these findings correspond to the assumptions from the partnering literature, which suggests that it is beneficial for construction firms to engage in close cooperation with other construction firms and/or subcontractors. On the other hand, the results strongly contradict the mainstream evidence of cross industrial studies that report long-term wealth destruction for bidders after an acquisition as Rau and Vermaelen (1998).

3.3.2 Strategic Focuses of Takeovers by Construction Firms

Though the results of the overall samples provide a first impression about the general long-term wealth effects for bidders in the construction industry, with the subsequent analysis I strive to illuminate the wealth effects for the various strategic focuses of these takeovers. At first, I discuss the horizontal, vertical and conglomerate acquisitions by construction firms. At horizontal acquisitions the abnormal returns amount to around 25%. All results are significant at the 1% level, regardless of the test procedure. The abnormal returns at vertical transactions depict clear significant wealth effects of 18% for the shareholder after the three years. The median takeover again does not seem to have a remarkable impact on corporate wealth. On horizontal acquisitions, construction firms only gain ca. 1% BHAR and on vertical transactions this amount shrinks even below 1%. Nevertheless, considering the percentage rate of takeovers with positive BHAR of up to 67% at horizontal and 70% at vertical acquisitions, both strategies entail positive wealth impacts for most bidding firms even though the effects might be small.

An extension towards other industries by conglomerate acquisitions also entails positive long-term wealth effects for construction firms. Acquirer gain BHAR of 21% from such acquisitions. Similar to vertical acquisitions the median transaction is only slightly above zero. Overall, the results from the takeovers classified according to their strategic focuses along the construction industry value chain indicate positive long-term wealth impacts for construction firms when increasing the critical aspect firm size and realizing cost synergies by horizontal takeovers or when extending their business value chain by vertical integration. All these positive effects fit to the described positive effects from partnering. The results support the assumption that construction firms not only benefit from cooperating with other construction firms or up- and downstream-related businesses, but also from integrating competitors, subcontractors or facility operators.

Table 3.4: BHAR of Horizontal, Vertical and Conglomerate Takeovers by Construction Firms

Horizontal; N=137	Mean	t-value	p-Value	Skewness Adjusted j-value	Skewness Adjusted p-value	Bootstrapped p-value	Median	Wilcoxon Z-Score	P-Value	Positives	Std. Dev.
One Year Event Period											
MV Portfolio	4.10%	1.620	10.99%	1.686**	9.65%	7.80%	-0.19%	-0.409	68.23%	41.18%	43.65%
MTBV Portfolio	12.06%	3.334***	0.13%	3.454***	0.09%	0.00%	0.81%	-3.348***	0.08%	65.82%	32.15%
Combined Portfolio	24.76%	5.922***	0.00%	6.050***	0.00%	0.00%	1.18%	-3.608***	0.03%	56.88%	20.87%
Two Years Event Period											
MV Portfolio	4.77%	1.682*	9.71%	1.755*	8.38%	6.90%	0.24%	-0.165	86.90%	52.94%	45.12%
MTBV Portfolio	12.77%	3.376***	0.11%	3.501***	0.08%	0.00%	1.28%	-4.633***	0.00%	67.09%	33.63%
Combined Portfolio	25.72%	5.953***	0.00%	6.084***	0.00%	0.00%	1.01%	-4.192***	0.00%	66.97%	23.37%
Three Years Event Period											
MV Portfolio	4.48%	1.653	10.30%	1.724*	8.93%	7.10%	-0.12%	-0.318	75.07%	45.59%	44.41%
MTBV Portfolio	12.38%	3.349***	0.13%	3.470***	0.09%	0.00%	0.94%	-4.183***	0.00%	68.35%	32.86%
Combined Portfolio	25.25%	5.037***	0.00%	6.067***	0.00%	0.00%	0.88%	3.850***	0.01%	61.47%	22.75%
Vertical; N=67											
One Year Event Period											
MV Portfolio	2.66%	0.992	32.79%	1.067	29.30%	25.20%	0.20%	-0.430	66.72%	54.05%	38.80%
MTBV Portfolio	13.85%	2.423**	2.06%	2.548**	1.52%	1.40%	0.26%	-1.788*	7.38%	59.46%	34.78%
Combined Portfolio	17.79%	3.431***	0.11%	3.555***	0.08%	0.10%	0.46%	-2.015**	4.39%	60.71%	16.33%
Two Years Event Period											
MV Portfolio	3.05%	1.117	27.15%	1.198	23.87%	20.80%	0.76%	-1.064	28.75%	62.16%	38.75%
MTBV Portfolio	14.77%	2.582**	1.40%	2.720***	0.99%	0.20%	0.73%	-2.783***	0.54%	72.97%	34.81%
Combined Portfolio	18.16%	3.507***	0.09%	3.634***	0.06%	0.00%	0.89%	-2.757***	0.58%	69.64%	16.63%
Three Years Event Period											
MV Portfolio	2.95%	1.093	28.15%	1.178	24.64%	22.70%	0.09%	-0.717	47.36%	54.05%	38.79%
MTBV Portfolio	14.51%	2.537**	1.57%	2.672**	1.13%	0.60%	0.43%	-2.542**	1.10%	64.86%	34.80%
Combined Portfolio	18.19%	3.509***	0.09%	3.637***	0.06%	0.00%	0.60%	-2.423**	1.54%	62.50%	16.40%
Difference Test	**1 Year:**			**2 Years:**			**3 Years:**				
Horizontal vs. Vertical	**t-value**	**z-score**		**t-value**	**z-score**		**t-value**	**z-score**			
MV Portfolio	0.363	0.472		0.395	0.243		0.367	0.472			
MTBV Portfolio	0.321	-0.510		0.346	-0.594		0.370	-0.401			
Combined Portfolio	1.008	-0.545		1.068	-0.680		1.009	-0.607			

Table 3.4 illustrates the average and medians of the buy-and-hold abnormal returns (BHAR) of 243 quoted construction firms worldwide, which underwent 137 horizontal, 67 vertical and 39 conglomerate takeovers in the period from 1985 until 2004. As reference portfolios serve rivals with similar market values, market-to-book values and a combination of these two criteria. The significance for the average BHAR values is tested with the t-test, the skewness-adjusted t-test and the bootstrapping procedure. The median BHAR values are tested with the Wilcoxon-Signed-Rank test. *, **, *** indicate the statistical significance to the 10%, 5% and 1% level, respectively. The Positive-Value refers to the percentage of takeovers with positive abnormal returns. The standard deviation refers to the volatility of the BHAR.

Table 3.4: BHAR of Horizontal, Vertical and Conglomerate Takeovers by Construction Firms – Continued

Conglomerate; N=39	**Mean**	**t-value**	**p-Value**	**Skewness Adjusted j-value**	**Skewness Adjusted p-value**	**Bootstrapped p-value**	**Median**	**Wilcoxon Z-Score**	**P-Value**	**Positives**	**Std. Dev.**
One Year Event Period											
MV Portfolio	-0.18%	0.172	86.51%	0.158	87.66%	88.10%	-0.31%	-0.849	39.58%	38.89%	41.43%
MTBV Portfolio	9.47%	1.429	16.88%	1.541	13.89%	13.40%	-0.37%	-0.365	71.51%	47.62%	30.39%
Combined Portfolio	20.77%	2.506**	1.94%	2.644**	1.42%	1.10%	0.27%	-1.547	12.18%	56.00%	4.34%
Two Years Event Period											
MV Portfolio	0.73%	0.647	52.63%	0.695	49.65%	49.70%	-0.34%	-0.806	42.04%	38.89%	42.70%
MTBV Portfolio	10.56%	1.475	15.59%	1.598	12.58%	10.40%	0.20%	-0.608	54.30%	52.38%	32.81%
Combined Portfolio	21.60%	2.529**	1.84%	2.671**	1.34%	0.00%	0.17%	-1.359	17.42%	56.00%	4.77%
Three Years Event Period											
MV Portfolio	0.30%	0.573	57.44%	0.597	55.83%	53.20%	-0.54%	-0.240	81.07%	38.89%	42.34%
MTBV Portfolio	10.43%	1.503	14.84%	1.630	11.87%	10.80%	0.57%	-1.477	13.96%	52.38%	31.78%
Combined Portfolio	21.09%	2.490**	2.01%	2.630**	1.47%	0.50%	0.70%	-2.005**	4.50%	56.00%	2.25%
Difference Test	**1 Year:**			**2 Years:**			**3 Years:**				
Horizontal vs. Conglomerate	**t-value**	**z-score**		**t-value**	**z-score**		**t-value**	**z-score**			
MV Portfolio	0.861	0.262		0.727	0.007		0.788	0.471			
MTBV Portfolio	0.332	-1.324		0.270	-1.502		0.244	-0.842			
Combined Portfolio	0.417	-0.109		0.416	-0.503		0.427	0.086			
Difference Test	**1 Year:**			**2 Years:**			**3 Years:**				
Vertical vs. Conglomerate	**t-value**	**z-score**		**t-value**	**z-score**		**t-value**	**z-score**			
MV Portfolio	0.722	-0.221		0.579	-0.819		0.678	-0.169			
MTBV Portfolio	0.514	-1.067		0.487	-1.183		0.477	-0.422			
Combined Portfolio	0.312	0.199		0.358	-0.118		0.302	0.343			

3.3.3 Detailed Analysis of Takeovers of Non-Construction Firms

As already introduced in chapter 3.1, there are several subcontractors extending their business into the construction business by purchasing a construction firm. The results for bidders integrating construction firms vertically illuminate BHAR of 24% over the 36 months observation period. Furthermore, the high rate of 69% of positive transactions supports the wealth-creating impact of vertical integration of construction firms. However, the low median values imply again skewed results. The few companies unrelated to the construction sector were able to realize on average abnormal returns of 57% from acquisitions of construction firms. With those returns, this subgroup outperforms all other forms of acquisitions within the construction industry. In addition, the median values of 17% stress the highly positive wealth effects for the main part of the acquisition, despite the mostly negative experience at conglomerate diversification (Berger and Ofek, 1995). Overall the purchase of essential construction knowledge and the increase in the flexibility of strategic decisions contributes positively to the performance of non-construction firms. It also increases the stability of the planning process construction project as no litigations or other disagreements with the operating construction firm have to be solved. Litigations do not only imply additional expenses for the company, but also jeopardizes the compliance with the timeline of the construction project. A delay in the finalization of a construction project often causes forfeits or a shortfall in revenues. A integration of a construction firm might avoid these potential risks.

The 15 financial institutions, in particular REITs as property related businesses yield more than 50% BHAR from acquisitions of construction firms within the 36 months observation period. These high returns are also reported for the median values. Due to the small sample size I can only cautiously interpret these findings. The results indicate a professional investment selection at the observed financial institutions and a strong capability to restructure construction firms efficiently can result in high profits in the long run.

The transactions exercised due to financial difficulties of the construction firm only show positive BHAR of 3% in the first 12 months after the acquisition. These results are surprising at first, as firms with financial problems are supposed to cause financial burdens for the acquiring company rather than yield financial benefits. Most probably the capital market assesses the acquisition of the construction firms with financial problems less burdensome than the expected credit defaults or the losses from the abandonment of an ongoing project. Therefore all savings interventions are positively rewarded in the first year after the event. When extending the observation period, the BHAR decline and become finally insignificant.

Table 3.5: BHAR of Vertical and Conglomerate Takeovers by Non-Construction Firms

Vertical; N=71	Mean	t-value	p-value	Skewness Adjusted j-value	Skewness Adjusted p-value	Bootstrapped p-value	Median	Wilcoxon z-score	P-value	Positives	Std. Dev.
12 Months Event Period											
MV Portfolio	15.30%	2.158**	3.96%	2.286**	3.00%	1.50%*	-0.09%	-1.114	26.53%	48.28%	44.59%
MTBV Portfolio	24.64%	2.932***	0.66%	3.062***	0.48%	0.30%***	-0.43%	-1.049	29.43%	44.83%	45.25%
Combined Portfolio	25.01%	3.020***	0.53%	3.157***	0.38%	0.30%***	0.87%	-2.087*	8.17%	62.07%	38.18%
24 Months Event Period											
MV Portfolio	14.84%	2.108**	4.41%	2.231**	3.39%	2.10%**	0.30%	-0.725	46.87%	55.17%	44.18%
MTBV Portfolio	24.23%	2.922***	0.68%	3.052***	0.49%	0.40%***	-0.05%	-0.746	45.56%	48.28%	44.65%
Combined Portfolio	24.49%	2.985***	0.58%	3.120***	0.42%	0.30%***	0.44%	-2.519**	1.18%	68.97%	37.91%
36 Months Event Period											
MV Portfolio	14.36%	2.121**	4.29%	2.245**.	3.28%	2.30%**	0.29%	-2.498**	1.85%	68.97%	43.92%
MTBV Portfolio	24.12%	2.940***	0.65%	3.071***	0.47%	0.30%***	0.26%	-1.503	13.29%	62.07%	44.18%
Combined Portfolio	24.33%	2.984***	0.58%	3.118***	0.42%	0.80%***	0.46%	-2.519**	1.18%	68.97%	36.45%
Congolmerate; N=17											
12 Months Event Period											
MV Portfolio	29.86%	1.565	16.85%	1.720	13.62%	10.60%	2.41%	—	—	57.14%	52.86%
MTBV Portfolio	30.63%	1.621	15.61%	1.785	12.45%	13.50%	2.41%	—	—	71.43%	49.98%
Combined Portfolio	56.36%	2.820**	3.03%	2.693**	3.59%	2.80%**	13.22%	—	—	71.43%	50.47%
24 Months Event Period											
MV Portfolio	29.27%	1.548	17.26%	1.701	13.99%	11.80%	0.06%	—	—	57.14%	53.54%
MTBV Portfolio	29.62%	1.572	16.69%	1.728	13.48%	15.90%	0.06%	—	—	57.14%	49.84%
Combined Portfolio	57.00%	2.816**	3.05%	2.684**	3.64%	2.60%**	17.00%	—	—	71.43%	50.02%
36 Months Event Period											
MV Portfolio	29.37%	1.584	16.44%	1.742	13.22%	11.50%	1.90%	—	—	57.14%	53.12%
MTBV Portfolio	29.30%	1.578	16.56%	1.735	13.34%	15.20%	1.90%	—	—	57.14%	49.13%
Combined Portfolio	57.18%	2.847**	2.93%	2.701**	3.51%	2.40%**	17.80%	—	—	71.43%	49.06%
Difference Test	**1 Year:**			**2 Years:**			**3 Years:**				
Vertical. vs. Conglomerate	**t-value**	**z-score**		**t-value**	**z-score**		**t-value**	**z-score**			
MV Portfolio	0.831	—		0.189	—		0.992	—			
MTBV Portfolio	0.080	—		0.125	—		0.164	—			
Combined Portfolio	0.137	0.201		0.155	0.101		0.149	0.302			

Table 3.5 illustrates the average and medians of the buy-and-hold abnormal returns (BHAR) of 88 quoted non-construction firms worldwide, which underwent vertical (71) or conglomerate (17) takeovers in the period from 1985 until 2004. As reference portfolios serve rivals with similar market values, market-to-book values and a combination of these two criteria. The significance for the average BHAR values is tested with the t-test, the skewness-adjusted t-test and the bootstrapping procedure. The median BHAR values are tested with the Wilcoxon-Signed-Rank test. *, **, *** indicate the statistical significance to the 10%, 5% and 1% level, respectively. The Positive-Value refers to the percentage of takeovers with positive abnormal returns. The standard deviation refers to the volatility of the BHAR.

Table 3.6: BHAR of Investment and Financial Difficulties Takeovers by Non-Construction Firms

Financial Investment; N=15	Mean	t-value	p-value	Skewness Adjusted j-value	Skewness Adjusted p-value	Bootstrapped p-value	Median	Wilcoxon z-score	P-value	Positives	Std. Dev.
12 Months Event Period											
MV Portfolio	24.79%	1.492	17.95%	1.641	14.48%	17.50%	1.15%	—	—	66.67%	55.83%
MTBV Portfolio	37.39%	1.984*	8.76%	2.093*	7.47%	6.80%*	0.55%	—	—	60.00%	53.31%
Combined Portfolio	50.78%	2.228*	7.63%	2.228*	6.63%	5.70%*	51.02%	—	—	86.67%	47.00%
24 Months Event Period											
MV Portfolio	25.46%	1.543	16.67%	1.701	13.27%	14.80%	0.44%	—	—	100.00%	55.69%
MTBV Portfolio	37.78%	2.012*	8.40%	2.124*	7.13%	6.10%*	0.77%	—	—	80.00%	53.09%
Combined Portfolio	51.03%	2.244*	7.48%	2.245*	6.48%	5.10%*	50.76%	—	—	100.00%	46.68%
36 Months Event Period											
MV Portfolio	25.56%	1.550	16.50%	1.710	13.10%	14.20%	0.74%	—	—	100.00%	55.63%
MTBV Portfolio	37.59%	1.995*	8.62%	2.105*	7.33%	6.30%*	0.38%	—	—	66.67%	53.29%
Combined Portfolio	51.13%	2.251*	7.41%	2.252*	6.41%	7.50%*	50.93%	—	—	100.00%	46.64%
Financial Difficulties N=8											
12 Months Event Period											
MV Portfolio	1.74%	2.669**	4.44%	2.711**	4.22%	3.30%**	1.52%	—	—	100.00%	39.02%
MTBV Portfolio	3.12%	4.619***	0.57%	3.678**	1.43%	3.10%**	3.43%	—	—	100.00%	44.52%
Combined Portfolio	2.67%	3.231**	2.32%	3.029**	2.91%	1.90%**	3.04%	—	—	100.00%	39.02%
24 Months Event Period											
MV Portfolio	0.22%	1.095	32.35%	1.132	30.87%	34.20%	0.12%	—	—	62.50%	38.81%
MTBV Portfolio	-0.11%	-0.205	84.59%	-0.250	81.25%	85.80%	0.30%	—	—	50.00%	44.19%
Combined Portfolio	-0.18%	-0.342	74.61%	-0.398	70.69%	68.70%	0.12%	—	—	25.00%	38.95%
36 Months Event Period											
MV Portfolio	-0.34%	-1.725	14.51%	-1.905	11.52%	13.60%	-0.31%	—	—	25.00%	38.25%
MTBV Portfolio	-0.97%	-1.069	33.38%	-1.254	26.54%	30.40%	-0.17%	—	—	50.00%	43.48%
Combined Portfolio	-1.13%	-1.256	26.45%	-1.473	20.08%	15.90%	-0.31%	—	—	25.00%	38.29%
Difference Test	**1 Year:**			**2 Years:**			**3 Years:**				
Investment vs. Fin.Dif.	**t-value**	**z-score**		**t-value**	**z-score**		**t-value**	**z-score**			
MV Portfolio	-1.376	—		0.161	—		1.706	—			
MTBV Portfolio	0.607	—		0.649	—		0.644	—			
Combined Portfolio	1.655	—		1.734	—		1.759	—			

Table 3.6 illustrates the average and medians of the buy-and-hold abnormal returns (BHAR) of 23 quoted non-construction firms worldwide, which acquired construction firms as a financial investment (15) or due to its financial instability (8) in the period from 1985 until 2004. As reference portfolios serve rivals with similar market values, market-to-book values and a combination of these two criteria. The significance for the average BHAR values is tested with the t-test, the skewness-adjusted t-test and the bootstrapping procedure. The median BHAR values are tested with the Wilcoxon-Signed-Rank test. *, **, *** indicate the statistical significance to the 10%, 5% and 1% level, respectively. The Positive-Value refers to the percentage of takeovers with positive abnormal returns. The standard deviation refers to the volatility of the BHAR.

3.3.4 Domestic and International Takeovers

Several construction firms distribute their business activities to various countries in order to reduce their economic dependency on one market and to scatter their revenue streams. International business expansion enables construction firms to benefit from the double-digit growth rates in construction volumes within the emerging economies like East Asia (McGraw-Hill, 2007). Foreign acquisitions permit companies to raise their international presence and business size, thereby enhancing their bidding position for large international projects (Seth et al., 2002). Furthermore, with the acquisition of a foreign firm, the acquirer also obtains the resources and knowledge for operating successfully under the specific business behavior and law requirements of the respective country (Conklin, 2005). Technological knowledge can also be transferred between the two parties, entailing advantage in comparison to the competitors (Morck and Yeung, 1991). On the other hand, international acquisitions bear high risks such as an underestimation of the foreign cultural differences as well as tremendous integration costs (Denis et al., 2002).

Construction firms benefit from international as well as domestic acquisitions. The international acquisitions yield BHAR of 25% to 22%, which are not significantly different from the domestic alternative. Non-construction bidders also gain at domestic takeovers only insignificantly lower BHAR (16%) than at international acquisitions (BHAR of 28%). The median values do not provide a valuable hint about the more favorable acquisition alternative, as all median BHAR amount to ca. 1%. Nevertheless, several countries like Ireland, Spain, the United Kingdom and the United States underwent a boom in the real estate sector and, subsequently, in the residential construction market from the mid-nineties through 2007. Due to the high growth expectations for these construction markets, domestic acquisitions in those countries might be superior to domestic takeovers in countries without real estate booms. While that phenomenon is of minor relevance for acquisitions by construction firms, as the BHAR values of both groups show similar results, it is highly relevant for takeovers by non-construction firms. Domestic acquisitions within the real estate booming countries yield around 30% BHAR. Also lower, the median values of 3% support the assumption of benefits for most bidders. Consequently, more than 58% of the non-construction firms yield positive BHAR when undergoing acquisitions in real estate boom markets. Domestic acquisitions in countries without strong growth rates in the real estate sector report results of slightly below zero. The median values show negative or minor positive results. The partly significant results from the difference test stress the strong difference between the BHAR of the two groups. Hence, it can be followed that the choice of the market for takeovers induces a significant impact for the accomplishment of abnormal returns for non-construction bidders.

Table 3.7: BHAR of International and Domestic Takeovers by Construction Firms

International; N=55	Mean	t-value	p-value	Skewness Adjusted j-value	Skewness Adjusted p-value	Bootstrapped p-value	Median	z-score	P-value	Positives	Std. Dev.
12 Months Event Period											
MV Portfolio	2.86%	0.746	46.24%	0.812	42.47%	40.20%	-0.76%	-1.308	19.09%	30.77%	43.69%
MTBV Portfolio	2.69%	0.826	41.56%	0.894	37.86%	36.90%	-0.25%	-0.833	40.48%	40.00%	17.83%
Combined Portfolio	24.15%	3.496***	0.12%	3.620***	0.08%	0.00%***	-0.07%	-1.384	16.62%	47.50%	19.51%
24 Months Event Period											
MV Portfolio	3.64%	0.972	34.02%	1.062	29.82%	26.80%	0.24%	-0.292	77.02%	57.69%	43.92%
MTBV Portfolio	3.83%	1.099	28.07%	1.200	23.98%	24.30%	0.44%	-1.244	21.34%	53.33%	19.10%
Combined Portfolio	25.18%	3.625***	0.08%	3.760***	0.06%	0.00%***	1.07%	-2.809	0.49%***	70.00%	19.11%
36 Months Event Period											
MV Portfolio	3.67%	0.973	33.98%	1.064	29.74%	27.40%	-0.07%	-0.013	98.99%	46.15%	43.84%
MTBV Portfolio	4.01%	1.170	25.16%	1.280	21.07%	19.20%	0.39%	-1.759	7.86%*	56.67%	18.76%
Combined Portfolio	25.05%	3.613***	0.09%	3.747***	0.06%	0.00%***	0.81%	-2.608	0.91%***	65.00%	19.25%
Domestic; N=188											
12 Months Event Period											
MV Portfolio	3.09%	1.727*	8.74%	1.788*	7.70%	8.60%*	-0.04%	-0.322	74.74%	48.45%	41.53%
MTBV Portfolio	14.92%	4.366***	0.00%	4.493***	0.00%	0.00%***	0.83%	-4.165	0.00%***	66.98%	35.19%
Combined Portfolio	21.66%	6.386***	0.00%	6.515***	0.00%	0.00%***	0.86%	-4.249	0.00%***	60.67%	17.63%
24 Months Event Period											
MV Portfolio	3.67%	1.813*	7.30%	1.880*	6.31%	5.30%*	0.11%	-0.480	63.10%	52.58%	42.79%
MTBV Portfolio	15.67%	4.425***	0.00%	4.556***	0.00%	0.00%***	1.03%	-5.189	0.00%***	69.81%	36.46%
Combined Portfolio	22.36%	6.399***	0.00%	6.528***	0.00%	0.00%***	0.85%	-4.459	0.00%***	65.33%	19.91%
36 Months Event Period											
MV Portfolio	3.34%	1.741*	8.50%	1.805*	7.42%	6.20%*	-0.20%	-0.221	82.49%	47.42%	42.21%
MTBV Portfolio	15.21%	4.367***	0.00%	4.495***	0.00%	0.00%***	0.88%	-4.764	0.00%***	66.98%	35.85%
Combined Portfolio	21.98%	6.377***	0.00%	6.505***	0.00%	0.00%***	0.71%	-4.209	0.00%***	60.00%	18.88%
Difference Test	**1 Year:**			**2 Years:**			**3 Years:**				
International vs. Domestic	**t-value**	**z-score**		**t-value**	**z-score**		**t-value**	**z-score**			
MV Portfolio	0.059	-0.286		0.005	0.137		-0.081	0.435			
MTBV Portfolio	1.835*	-2.732***		1.710*	-1.771*		1.646	-1.079			
Combined Portfolio	0.333	-0.814		0.368	0.422		-0.406	0.205			

Table 3.7 illustrates the average and medians of the buy-and-hold abnormal returns (BHAR) of 243 quoted construction firms worldwide, which underwent 55 international and 188 domestic takeovers in the period from 1985 until 2004. As reference portfolios serve rivals with similar market values, market-to-book values and a combination of these two criteria. The significance for the average BHAR values is tested with the t-test, the skewness-adjusted t-test and the bootstrapping procedure. The median BHAR values are tested with the Wilcoxon-Signed-Rank test. *, **, *** indicate the statistical significance to the 10%, 5% and 1% level, respectively. The Positive-Value refers to the percentage of takeovers with positive abnormal returns. The standard deviation refers to the volatility of the BHAR.

Table 3.8: BHAR of International and Domestic Takeovers by Non-Construction Firms

International; N=39	Mean	t-value	p-value	Skewness Adjusted j-value	Skewness Adjusted p-value	Bootstrapped p-value	Median	z-score	P-value	Positives	Std. Dev.
12 Months Event Period											
MV Portfolio	17.82%	1.945*	6.85%	2.093*	5.17%	3.40%**	0.69%	-1.809*	7.04%	61.11%	45.89%
MTBV Portfolio	28.80%	2.644**	1.70%	2.788**	1.26%	2.20%**	0.96%	-2.243**	2.49%	66.67%	46.21%
Combined Portfolio	28.59%	2.643**	1.71%	2.787**	1.26%	1.20%**	0.71%	-2.417**	1.89%	72.22%	38.87%
24 Months Event Period											
MV Portfolio	17.09%	1.861*	8.01%	1.999*	6.18%	4.20%**	0.26%	-1.765	7.75%	72.22%	45.85%
MTBV Portfolio	27.68%	2.540**	2.11%	2.675**	1.60%	2.40%**	0.57%	-1.746	7.77%	66.67%	46.23%
Combined Portfolio	27.70%	2.563**	2.02%	2.701**	1.52%	1.10%**	0.30%	-2.156**	4.75%	77.78%	38.95%
36 Months Event Period											
MV Portfolio	17.06%	1.873*	7.84%	2.013*	6.03%	4.10%**	0.57%	-2.507**	1.22%	77.78%	46.23%
MTBV Portfolio	27.79%	2.532**	2.15%	2.665**	1.63%	2.50%**	0.44%	-1.938*	5.26%	72.22%	46.58%
Combined Portfolio	27.97%	2.567**	2.00%	2.704**	1.51%	0.60%***	0.52%	-2.635**	1.08%	77.78%	38.65%
Domestic; N=72											
12 Months Event Period											
MV Portfolio	17.27%	2.464**	1.97%	2.599**	1.44%	0.80%***	1.01%	-2.215**	2.68%	64.52%	39.02%
MTBV Portfolio	23.27%	2.910***	0.67%	3.041***	0.49%	0.10%***	0.40%	-1.489	13.64%	51.61%	44.52%
Combined Portfolio	17.48%	2.493**	1.84%	2.629**	1.34%	0.70%***	1.15%	-2.058**	3.96%	64.52%	39.02%
24 Months Event Period											
MV Portfolio	16.59%	2.371**	2.44%	2.496**	1.83%	1.20%**	0.30%	-1.647*	9.97%	64.52%	38.81%
MTBV Portfolio	22.83%	2.876***	0.73%	3.005***	0.53%	0.10%***	-0.19%	-0.647	51.78%	48.39%	44.19%
Combined Portfolio	16.82%	2.413**	2.21%	2.541**	1.64%	2.80%**	0.36%	-1.333	12.64%	58.06%	38.95%
36 Months Event Period											
MV Portfolio	16.24%	2.361**	2.49%	2.485**	1.87%	1.00%***	0.11%	-1.313	18.91%	61.29%	38.25%
MTBV Portfolio	22.47%	2.878***	0.73%	3.006***	0.53%	0.20%***	0.01%	-0.568	56.98%	51.61%	43.48%
Combined Portfolio	16.21%	2.359**	2.50%	2.483**	1.88%	1.10%**	0.11%	-1.333	18.27%	58.06%	38.29%
Difference Test	**1 Year:**			**2 Years:**			**3 Years:**				
International vs. Domestic	**t-value**	**z-score**		**t-value**	**z-score**		**t-value**	**z-score**			
MV Portfolio	0.860	—		0.112	—		-1.033	—			
MTBV Portfolio	-1.501	1.775		-1.457	1.323		-1.483	1.388			
Combined Portfolio	-1.184	0.642		-1.187	0.688		-1.259	1.560			

Table 3.8 illustrates the average and medians of the buy-and-hold abnormal returns (BHAR) of 111 quoted non-A158construction firms worldwide, which underwent 39 international and 72 domestic takeovers in the construction industry in the period from 1985 until 2004. As reference portfolios serve rivals with similar market values, market-to-book values and a combination of these two criteria. The significance for the average BHAR values is tested with the t-test, the skewness-adjusted t-test and the bootstrapping procedure. The median BHAR values are tested with the Wilcoxon-Signed-Rank test. *, **, *** indicate the statistical significance to the 10%, 5% and 1% level, respectively. The Positive-Value refers to the percentage of takeovers with positive abnormal returns. The standard deviation refers to the volatility of the BHAR.

Table 3.9: Detailed BHAR Analysis of Domestic Takeovers by Construction Firms

Domestic Takeovers within E, IRL, UK, US; N=128	Mean	t-value	p-value	Skewness Adjusted j-value	Skewness Adjusted p-value	Bootstrapped p-value	Median	z-score	P-value	Positives	Std. Dev.
12 Months Event Period											
MV Portfolio	2.78%	1.252	21.49%	1.307	19.59%	17.60%	-0.13%	-0.195	84.55%	43.94%	40.69%
MTBV Portfolio	15.23%	3.608***	0.06%	3.740***	0.04%	0.00%***	1.18%	-4.028***	0.01%	71.83%	35.56%
Combined Portfolio	19.74%	4.900***	0.00%	5.022***	0.00%	0.00%***	0.43%	-2.696***	0.70%	55.88%	18.04%
24 Months Event Period											
MV Portfolio	3.24%	1.421	16.00%	1.487	14.18%	13.10%	0.08%	-0.176	86.06%	51.52%	40.78%
MTBV Portfolio	15.57%	3.686***	0.04%	3.822***	0.03%	0.10%***	1.25%	-4.647***	0.00%	73.24%	35.61%
Combined Portfolio	20.06%	4.967***	0.00%	5.092***	0.00%	0.00%***	0.74%	-2.866***	0.42%	62.75%	18.52%
36 Months Event Period											
MV Portfolio	3.06%	1.390	16.92%	1.456	15.03%	15.10%	-0.41%	-0.335	73.73%	48.48%	40.47%
MTBV Portfolio	15.12%	3.612***	0.06%	3.744***	0.04%	0.10%***	0.93%	-4.252***	0.00%	69.01%	35.28%
Combined Portfolio	19.91%	4.969***	0.00%	5.095***	0.00%	0.00%***	0.60%	-2.806***	0.50%	59.80%	17.91%
Domestic Takeovers excluding E, IRL, UK, US; N=60											
12 Months Event Period											
MV Portfolio	3.75%	1.229	22.85%	1.336	19.15%	17.80%	0.09%	-0.882	37.79%	58.06%	43.42%
MTBV Portfolio	14.31%	2.423**	2.09%	2.550**	1.55%	1.70%**	0.40%	-1.638	10.14%	57.14%	34.94%
Combined Portfolio	25.73%	4.105***	0.02%	4.247***	0.01%	0.00%***	1.43%	-3.487***	0.05%	70.83%	17.00%
24 Months Event Period											
MV Portfolio	4.57%	1.112	27.52%	1.207	23.69%	19.80%	0.26%	-1.019	30.82%	54.84%	46.85%
MTBV Portfolio	15.87%	2.428**	2.06%	2.558**	1.52%	1.30%**	0.86%	-2.391**	1.68%	62.86%	38.67%
Combined Portfolio	27.25%	4.029***	0.02%	4.168***	0.01%	0.00%***	1.04%	-3.641***	0.03%	70.83%	22.89%
36 Months Event Period											
MV Portfolio	3.92%	1.033	30.99%	1.123	27.04%	26.80%	-0.12%	-0.803	42.17%	45.16%	45.82%
MTBV Portfolio	15.38%	2.426**	2.07%	2.555**	1.53%	1.10%**	0.55%	-2.195**	2.82%	62.86%	37.52%
Combined Portfolio	26.37%	3.987***	0.02%	4.122***	0.02%	0.10%***	1.24%	-3.272***	0.11%	60.42%	21.12%
Difference Test	**1 Year:**			**2 Years:**			**3 Years:**				
Domestics	**t-value**	**z-score**		**t-value**	**z-score**		**t-value**	**z-score**			
MV Portfolio	-0.251	0.601		-0.305	0.244		-0.206	0.284			
MTBV Portfolio	0.125	-1.064		-0.038	-0.910		-0.034	-0.863			
Combined Portfolio	-0.822	-0.414		-0.959	0.845		-0.873	0.628			

Table 3.9 illustrates the average and medians of the buy-and-hold abnormal returns (BHAR) of 188 quoted construction firms worldwide, which underwent domestic takeovers in countries with a real estate boom (128) and without a real estate boom (60) in the period from 1985 until 2004. As reference portfolios serve rivals with similar market values, market-to-book values and a combination of these two criteria. The significance for the average BHAR values is tested with the t-test, the skewness-adjusted t-test and the bootstrapping procedure. The median BHAR values are tested with theWilcoxon-Signed-Rank test. *, **, *** indicate the statistical significance to the 10%, 5% and 1% level, respectively. The Positive-Value refers to the percentage of takeovers with positive abnormal returns. The standard deviation refers to the volatility of the BHAR.

Table 3.10: Detailed BHAR Analysis of Domestic Takeovers by Non-Construction Firms

Domestic Takeovers within E, IRL, UK, US; N=33	Mean	t-value	p-value	Skewness Adjusted j-value	Skewness Adjusted p-value	Bootstrapped p-value	Median	z-score	P-value	Positives	Std. Dev.
12 Months Event Period											
MV Portfolio	44.74%	3.488***	0.30%	3.587***	0.25%	0.10%***	3.43%	-3.390***	0.07%	88.24%	48.79%
MTBV Portfolio	42.79%	3.326***	0.43%	3.413***	0.36%	0.10%***	3.43%	-2.249**	2.45%	64.71%	53.04%
Combined Portfolio	31.59%	2.669**	1.68%	2.810**	1.26%	0.90%***	2.92%	-2.961**	1.77%	70.59%	52.87%
24 Months Event Period											
MV Portfolio	43.31%	3.347***	0.41%	3.438***	0.34%	0.20%***	0.83%	-2.537**	2.12%	70.59%	48.45%
MTBV Portfolio	42.29%	3.315***	0.44%	3.402***	0.36%	0.50%***	0.83%	-1.682*	9.27%	52.94%	52.60%
Combined Portfolio	30.97%	2.635**	1.80%	2.774**	1.35%	0.50%***	0.62%	-2.140**	3.95%	58.82%	53.36%
36 Months Event Period											
MV Portfolio	42.14%	3.328***	0.43%	3.416***	0.35%	0.20%***	0.11%	-1.304	19.23%	58.82%	47.62%
MTBV Portfolio	41.65%	3.319***	0.43%	3.406***	0.36%	0.30%***	0.26%	-1.675*	9.39%	58.82%	51.73%
Combined Portfolio	30.30%	2.623**	1.84%	2.762**	1.39%	0.60%***	0.40%	-1.734*	8.40%	58.82%	52.20%
Domestic Takeovers excluding E, IRL, UK, US; N=39											
12 Months Event Period											
MV Portfolio	-0.35%	-0.860	40.54%	-0.877	39.67%	43.10%	-0.15%	0.663	70.56%	50.00%	2.63%
MTBV Portfolio	-0.79%	-1.232	23.96%	-1.208	24.85%	20.90%	-0.67%	1.224	17.26%	28.57%	2.39%
Combined Portfolio	0.34%	0.487	63.43%	0.488	63.36%	59.30%	0.63%	0.739	54.16%	57.14%	1.50%
24 Months Event Period											
MV Portfolio	0.13%	0.468	64.78%	0.473	64.39%	68.50%	0.19%	0.887	48.74%	64.29%	2.58%
MTBV Portfolio	-1.17%	-2.067*	5.92%	-2.126*	5.32%	3.60%**	-1.04%	1.732*	7.85%	35.71%	2.12%
Combined Portfolio	-0.36%	-0.520	61.20%	-0.528	60.63%	55.60%	0.19%	0.386	90.32%	57.14%	1.00%
36 Months Event Period											
MV Portfolio	0.19%	0.846	41.28%	0.866	40.22%	43.60%	0.19%	1.082	28.66%	71.43%	3.11%
MTBV Portfolio	-1.49%	-1.948*	7.33%	-2.111*	5.47%	3.80%**	-0.97%	1.859*	6.76%	35.71%	2.87%
Combined Portfolio	-0.89%	-1.076	30.15%	-1.142	27.40%	25.30%	0.06%	0.503	85.52%	57.14%	0.83%
Difference Test	**1 Year:**			**2 Years:**			**3 Years:**				
Domestics	**t-value**	**z-score**		**t-value**	**z-score**		**t-value**	**z-score**			
MV Portfolio	1.145	—		-0.653	—		-1.952	—			
MTBV Portfolio	1.162	1.674		1.161	2.830***		1.176	2.149**			
Combined Portfolio	2.114**	—		2.077*	—		2.077*	—			

Table 3.10 illustrates the average and medians of the buy-and-hold abnormal returns (BHAR) of 72 quoted non-construction firms worldwide, which underwent domestic takeovers in the construction industry in countries with a real estate boom (33) and without a real estate boom (39) in the period from 1985 until 2004. As reference portfolios serve rivals with similar market values, market-to-book values and a combination of these two criteria. The significance for the average BHAR values is tested with the t-test, the skewness-adjusted t-test and the bootstrapping procedure. The median BHAR values are tested with theWilcoxon-Signed-Rank test. *, **, *** indicate the statistical significance to the 10%, 5% and 1% level, respectively. The Positive-Value refers to the percentage of takeovers with positive abnormal returns. The standard deviation refers to the volatility of the BHAR.

3.4 Success Parameters of Takeovers

Firm and transaction characteristics often have an essential impact on the success of takeovers. The same accounts for certain macroeconomic circumstances, as the previous chapter illustrates. To illuminate the influence of these potential influence factors, I detect distinct parameters and investigate by the means of a multivariate regression analysis their positive or negative effect on the long-term abnormal returns. As throughout the entire study, I distinguish between the impact on takeovers by construction and non-construction firms.

i) Firm Specifics of the Acquirer

1. Leverage: Bruner (1988) reports rising leverage levels at bidding companies within the first two years after transactions, as debt capital is a common source for financing the transaction. Firms with high leverage levels usually spend less in R&D, thereby affecting negatively the basis for growth opportunities and the future performance (Singh and Faircloth, 2005).

2. Earnings per Share (EPS-ratio): Well-performing firms with high EPS-ratios usually indicate a shareholder-oriented management. Hence, the capital market expects further benefits from M&A activism, as the management is supposed to act in the shareholders' interest (Morck et al., 1990).

3. Tobin's Q: The Tobin's Q presented by Lang and Stulz (1994) allows examining the capability of a management to lead a company successfully on the current and future status. I test whether good management capabilities (Tobin's Q > 1) have an essential role on the success of takeovers.

ii) Transaction Characteristics

4. Strategic Focus: Considering the findings of the strategic focuses in chapter 3.3, I test whether those strategic focuses also influence significantly the BHAR in combination with other potential explanatory variables.

5. Domestic vs. International: Likewise to the strategic focuses, I analyze the effect of the geographical focus on the BHAR under the consideration of multiple exogenous variables. Similar to the procedure in the sub-sample analysis, I include a variable for all domestic as well as international acquisitions. Additionally, I split up the group of domestic acquisitions in the construction booming countries to consider the impact of that specific group within the domestic acquisitions.

6. Private vs. Public Targets: Takeovers of private targets usually serve more the shareholder wealth than acquisitions of public targets, because the valuation of private targets leads often to a discount of more than 15% in comparison to similar public companies (Officer, 2007). Fuller et al. (2002) support this thesis, as they report bidder gains at acquisitions of private targets, but discounts when acquiring publicly listed firms.

7. Hostile vs. Friendly Takeovers: In friendly takeovers, the target management agrees on the transaction, which avoids resistance during the integration process into the bidding company and any premium payments due to bidding competitions. In contrast, in hostile acquisitions acquirers often face a bidding competition and consequently premium payments as well as cultural barriers at the target. This causes higher costs and lower gains for the bidder during the integration process (De et al., 1996). Sudarsanam and Mahate (2006) state that hostile acquisitions outperform the friendly counterpart as hostile acquisitions often focus on underperforming targets. Also, the monitoring and corporate governance is improved at the target, in order to increase the shareholder value.

8. Method of Payment: Loughran and Vijh (1997) document significantly negative returns of -25% for only stock acquisitions and 61.7% abnormal returns for cash-financed acquisitions on a five-year horizon after the transaction. In addition to these two forms of payment, I also consider transactions using a mix of stock and cash for paying the acquisition.

iii) Macroeconomic Aspects and Capital Market Information

9. High M&A Activity: During the new economy hype and the stock market exaggeration at the end of the last millennium, the number of M&A increased too. During high M&A activities managers often feel the urge to merge instead of thoroughly understanding the acquisition benefits and drawbacks, because the market appears to be advantageous for M&A activities. In the short run, high M&A activities and stock market exaggerations benefit the bidder, but in the long run, those acquisitions often prove to be wealth deteriorating (Petmezas, 2009).

10. GDP and Real Estate Cycles: GDP development and real estate cycles are closely linked (Case et al., 2000). Hence, the GDP variable does not only provide information about the impact of the general macroeconomic development on the acquirer success, but also about the effect of development in the real estate business on the BHAR of acquisitions within the construction industry.

11. Short-Term Cumulated Abnormal Returns (CAR): If capital markets correspond to the efficiency thesis by Fama (1992), short-term abnormal returns should significantly affect long-term abnormal returns.

The regression analysis reveals that friendly and hostile acquisitions, stock payments and a general high activity of M&A influence significantly the long-term success of takeovers by construction firms. Friendly acquisitions seem to realize synergies and suffer less from high integration costs and transaction premiums than hostile acquisitions. Coinciding with the hypothesis by De et al. (1996), friendly acquisitions have a positive impact and the hostile counterpart a negative impact on the shareholder wealth. Unlike the findings of Loughran and Vijh (1997), stock-financed acquisitions have a positive effect on the accomplished long-term BHAR. Due to the financially scarce situation, construction firms require sufficient liquidity to overcome periods with weak revenues (Rice, 2007). Therefore, the capital market might prefer a payment by stocks than by cash. According to Petmezas (2009), construction firms lose in the long run when engaging in acquisitions during high M&A activities. This is mainly due to the paid high prices and premiums in these periods.

Table 3.11: Long-Term Regression Results for Construction Firms

Explanatory Variables	M1	M2	M3	M4	M5	M6	M7
Constant	0.185**	0.0599	0.413***	0.328***	0.336***	0.319***	0.139
	(-2.235)	(1.1419)	(4.226)	(3.876)	(3.212)	(3.601)	(1.625)
Leverage		-0.000				-0.000	
		(-0.172)				(-0.122)	
EPS		-0.001			-0.000		-0.001
		(-0.484)			(-0.637)		(-0.793)
Tobin's Q	-0.019		-0.035		-0.039		-0.038
	(-1.285)		(-1.593)		(-1.152)		(-1.182)
Domestic	-0.055					-0-041	
	(-0.822)					(-0.629)	
Domestic IRL,E,UK,US			-0.108*	-0.082			-0.103
			(-1.681)	(-1.329)			(-1.595)
International		0.051			0.041		
		(0.8058)			(0.632)		
Friendly	0.222***	0.184***					0.197***
	(5.477)	(4.597)					(3.838)
Hostile			-0.192***		-0.185***	-0.230***	
			(-3.444)		(-4.145)	(-5.813)	
Cash Financed			-0.077	-0.054			
			(-1.143)	(-0.860)			
Stock Financed		0.173**			0.141*		0.177**
		(2.073)			(1.723)		(2.152)
Cash/Stock Financed	-0.067					-0.060	
	(-0.817)					(-0.832)	
Private					-0.057		
					(-0.905)		
Public				0.028			
				(0.435)			
Horizontal (Constr.)			0.101*			0.030	0.083
			(1.709)			(0.535)	(1.348)
Vertical (Constr.)		-0.024		-0.006			
		(-0.287)		(-0.077)			
Conglomerate (Constr.)	-0.083				-0.099		
	(-1.121)				(-1.464)		
GDP		-0.007			-0.001	-0.002	
		(-0.512)			(-0.690)	(-1.167)	
Stock Market Bubble			-0.183***	-0.135**	-0.127**		0.177**
			(-2.956)	(-2.210)	(-2.220)		(2.152)
CAR short Analysis			0.131	0.203			
			0.132	(1.138)			
Durbin-Watson	2.223	2.226	2.227	2.290	2.198	2.192	2.236
Adj. R^Square	0.062	0.072	0.092	0.037	0.079	0.026	0.111
N Obs	198	197	198	216	198	237	182

Table 3.11 illustrates the results of the multivariate linear regression model for the three-year buy and hold abnormal returns of acquiring construction firms. *, **, *** indicate the statistical significance to the 10%, 5% and 1% level, respectively. The number in brackets presents the t-statistics. All test statistics are computed applying White's (1980) heteroskedasticity-consistent covariance matrix.

Table 3.12: Long-Term Regression Results for Non-Construction Firms

Explanatory Variables	M1	M2	M3	M4	M5	M6	M7
Constant	0.163	-0.111	0.184	0.556**	-0.008	0.026	-0.125
	(1.135)	(-1.228)	(1.914)	(2.097)	(-0.082)	(0.289)	(-1.348)
Leverage	-0.001**	-0.001***		-0.001**		-0.001***	-0.001***
	(-2.304)	(-2.607)		(-2.330)		(-2.683)	(-2.704)
EPS	0.022***	0.024***	0.024***		0.026***	0.017**	0.025
	(2.953)	(3.343)	(3.089)		(4.027)	(2.233)	(3.688)
Tobin's Q	0.001	0.001					
	(1.460)	(1.357)					
Domestic		0.251**			0.209*		0.279***
		(2.353)			(1.737)		(2.721)
Domestic IRL,E,UK,US			-0.037				
			(-0.297)				
International	-0.211			-0.216			
	(-1.562)			(-1.461)			
Friendly							
Hostile	0.040						
	(0.185)						
Cash Financed						-0.045	
						(-0.336)	
Stock Financed	-0.048						
	(-0.336)						
Cash/Stock Financed			0.026				
			(0.177)				
Private			-0.057	-0.014			
			(-0.484)	(-0.116)			
Public	-0.020					0.018	
	(-0.161)					(0.146)	
Vertical (Non-Constr.)		0.171*				0.319***	
		(1.759)				(2.891)	
Conglomerate (Non-Constr.)	-0.174					0.184	
	(-1.022)					(1.501)	
Financial Investment			0.346**		0.315***		
			(2.537)		(2.821)		
Financial Instability				-0.381**	-0.163*		
				(-2.271)	(-1.864)		
GDP	-0.001			-0.002			
	(-0.356)			(-0.612)			
Stock Market Bubble	0.115						
	(0.706)						
CAR shortterm Analysis		0.623*	0.719*		0.812*		0.775**
		(1.704)	(1.694)		1.939		(2.180)
Durbin-Watson	1.966	1.919	2.018	1.804	2.056	1.817	1.895
Adj. R^Square	0.174	0.291	0.135	0.077	0.198	0.182	0.293
N Obs	87	89	87	83	88	87	94

Table 3.12 illustrates the results of the multivariate linear regression model for the three-year buy and hold abnormal returns of acquiring non-construction firms. *, **, *** indicate the statistical significance to the 10%, 5% and 1% level, respectively. The number in brackets presents the t-statistics. All test statistics are computed applying White's (1980) heteroskedasticity-consistent covariance matrix.

All remaining introduced exogenous variables are of minor importance for the stock price performance. This also accounts for the various strategic, the national and the international diversification variables. Only horizontal acquisitions show at least a low significance in one regression, indicating a positive effect from the size increase for construction firms. Finally, domestic takeovers in countries with a real estate boom also report a negative impact in one regression. This might indicate that the expected benefits from intensifying the business in such countries by M&A reverse in a performance discount for the acquirer.

The regression results of the bidding non-construction firms illustrate an influence on the long-term takeover success by the following variables: Leverage, EPS, domestic focus, vertical focus, financial investment focus, financial instability focus and the CAR values of the short-term analysis. The impact of the three strategic focuses on the long-term M&A success of non-construction firms support the findings from the sub-sample analysis in chapter 3.3: An extension of the value chain by integrating an upstream or downstream construction business and financial investments into the construction industry influence positively excess gains for the acquirer, but takeovers due to financial difficulties of the construction firm entail financial burdens for the acquirer in the long run. In addition, the positive wealth effects from domestic acquisition analysis are underlined by the regression results.

The performance of the bidding company is another significant aspect for the accomplishment of excess long-term returns. In line with Morck et al. (1990), the capital market considers well-performing bidders as shareholder-oriented firms. Hence, from the management of those firms it is expected to pursue shareholder value increasing goals with an acquisition instead of fulfilling personal goals. On the other hand, high leverage ratios bear a devaluation threat for the shareholders of the bidding non-construction company in the long run. Singh and Faircloth (2005) assume a high level of debts jeopardize the long-term growth and profit situation of a firm, as cash inflows are required to fulfill the debt service instead of using them for required investments or as dividends.

Finally, the calculated short-term cumulated abnormal returns are reliable indicators for the long-term success of the acquisition by non-construction firms. This finding supports the market efficiency thesis by Fama (1992), who expects an immediate incorporation of new information into the stock prices. It also supports his thesis that long-term anomalies do not abandon the market efficiency hypothesis (Fama, 1998).

3.5 Conclusion

This study illustrates the long-term wealth effects of acquisitions within the construction industry. The partnering research in the construction industry provides first implications about the benefits and moral hazard risk avoidance due to cooperation between construction firms or between construction firms and their subcontractors. These insights and the introduced specifics of the construction industry suggest, in contrast to the findings of cross-industry studies, long-term excess yields for acquisitions within the construction industry. By measuring buy and hold abnormal returns and testing the results with the various significance tests, it shows that M&A activities have overall a positive impact on the shareholder value of the bidding company on a 12-, 24- and 36-months perspective, after the acquisition announcement. Construction firms yield average abnormal returns of 23% and non-construction firms of 21% over a three-year horizon.

By classifying overall sample according to the strategic focuses of the acquisition, a distinct picture arises. Construction bidders gain mainly from business size increasing horizontal acquisitions (26% BHAR). Nevertheless, vertical and conglomerate acquisitions also increase the shareholder value with maximum abnormal returns of 18% and 21% respectively. Hence, an increase of the company size by horizontal acquisitions, an enlargement towards up- or downstream-related businesses as well as extensions towards construction-alien business seem to benefit the shareholders of construction firms. A similar picture can be drawn for the acquisition by non-construction firms. Those businesses integrating vertically a construction firm yield BHAR of 24%. Non-construction firms using the acquisition as a financial investment accomplish BHAR of 51%, and companies not related to the construction industry even yield 57% BHAR by incorporating construction services into their company. Only the acquisitions caused by financial problems of the construction firms and a consequent failure of an ongoing project or big credit positions at a bank lead to negative BHAR of -1%.

The domestic or international focus seems for construction bidders of minor relevance as the results provide an inconsistent picture. For non-construction firms, the country of the acquisition is of major relevance. While domestic acquisitions in a country with a booming construction sector contribute a significant impact to the shareholder wealth increase (BHAR 30%), domestic acquisitions destroy in countries without a real estate boom shareholder value. In addition, the capital market rewards international diversification with BHAR of 29%.

The regression analysis reveals insights about the success parameters of takeovers within the construction industry. As expected from prior empirical studies, friendly acquisitions influence positively the acquisition success and hostile acquisitions negatively. This is due to the high bidder premiums and excessive integration costs at hostile acquisitions. Construction firms purchasing another company by a stock swap affect positively the long-term shareholder wealth, as they do not tighten the scarce liquidity situation at their firms. However, construction firms undergoing acquisitions in the urge to merge due to a general high M&A activity seem to overpay for the target and to destroy shareholder wealth in the long run.

At non-construction firms, the capital structure and the performance of the bidding firms significantly affect the transaction success. High-leveraged companies engaging in acquisitions obstruct their future growth. Therefore, the capital market evaluates acquisitions by such firms negatively, but rewards, on the other hand, acquisitions by well-performing firms. Those companies act in favor of the shareholder wealth, which includes profitable investments like acquisitions. In addition, the regression results partly underline the positive findings for the strategic and geographical focuses of the acquisitions. Finally, this study partly supports the market efficiency thesis by Fama (1992), as the regression result of the non-construction firms document a significant impact of short-term on long-term abnormal returns.

4 The Deteriorating Wealth Effect of National Acquisitions in Fragmented and Declining Markets

Abstract

The majority of M&A research documents positive bidder wealth effects from horizontal acquisitions within the domestic market. These findings also account for acquisitions conducted in declining national markets. Increasing market dominance and the option to redeploy resources efficiently explain these benefits. Nevertheless, I argue that in declining markets, in combination with a high level of fragmentation, these benefits are not achieved, and corporate wealth is destroyed.

Because the German construction industry saw a high fragmentation and decreasing market volumes in the period 1995–2004, I use this market for the analysis. Within the market I investigate the third biggest German construction firm, the Walter Bau AG, which uses domestic horizontal acquisitions to realize redeployment synergy yields and to strengthen its market position in the declining market. I show that the expected positive impacts from these transactions vanish quickly and that detrimental wealth effects result for the Walter Bau AG.

4.1 Introduction

In the period 1988–2008, the worldwide M&A transaction volume rose by 227% from a total value of 868bn USD to 2,842bn USD. Not surprisingly, extensive studies have addressed the question of the wealth effect for shareholders in relation to mergers and acquisitions (M&A). Most studies document strong positive yields for the target shareholders around the announcement of the acquisition (Jovanovic and Barguinsky, 2004; Campa and Hernando, 2004; Danbolt, 2003; Andrade et al., 2001). Contrarily, the results for the shareholder value of the acquirers draw an unspecific picture. Most recent studies either report negative wealth impacts for the bidders or no significant value effects at all from acquisitions. Moeller et al. (2005) describe for the period from 1998 to 2001 a total value destruction for bidding companies of 240bn USD, which are not transferred to the target shareholders. De Long (2001) displays negative CAR of -1.68% for the acquirers, and Houston et al. (2001) even document negative impacts of -3.47% around the acquisition announcements.

On the other hand, many studies, such as those by Campa and Hernando (2004 and 2006) as well as Beitel et al. (2004), present abnormal returns close to zero, indicating no specific wealth effect for the bidders. In contrast to these findings, Moeller et al. (2004) report positive yields for acquirers. Their results change, however, to negative yields when the sample is weighted according to its company market values. Regarding these results, M&A transactions seem mostly value destructive or at least not value enhancing for the acquiring company. However, when analyzing the acquisitions in detail and by focusing on the strategic and geographical direction of the takeover, a more distinct picture shows up for the acquirer share performance. According to Santos et al. (2008), the capital market disregards international acquisitions to unrelated business fields with an average discount of -24%. Lins and Servaes (1999) and Berger and Ofek (1995) support this finding, as they report for business diversifying acquisitions valuation discounts for the acquirer of -13% to -15%. The reasoning behind this is the lack of potential synergy effects and the risk of cross-subsidization of low-performing units by profitable divisions under the coverage of the conglomerate. However, the authors report far less value-destructive effects for related transactions. Not surprisingly, most studies on horizontal acquisitions demonstrate welfare gains for the bidding companies (Goergen and Renneborg, 2004; Pesendorfer, 2003; Levin and Peck, 2003). Horizontal mergers and acquisitions provide the involved parties with high synergy potentials and the opportunity to raise the market power. They are subsequently positively rewarded by the capital market. Campa and Hernando (2004) further argue that national horizontal acquisitions lead to higher market concentration and realize more easily the benefits resulting from a market dominating position. Furthermore, low cultural and legal barriers at domestic acquisitions usually allow the bidding companies to integrate the target firm rapidly and at lower costs as international targets. In contrast to these findings, some authors highlight the benefits from international diversification. Nadolska and Barkema (2007) describe the opportunity to boost the growth velocity of the firm by entering foreign markets and gaining new customers. Morrow et al. (2007) see in times of the accelerating global integration of most countries a need by the companies to extend their business to an international level to maintain their competitiveness and performance. Therefore, companies increasingly invest abroad either by setting up a subsidiary, by partnering with foreign firms, by alliances or by engaging in an acquisition of a foreign company (Collins and Hitt, 2006). Supported are those arguments by Santos et al. (2008), who provide evidence for no value destruction through related international acquisitions.

Nevertheless, studies comparing domestic and international acquisitions generally stress the superiority of domestic to international acquisitions (Denis et al., 2002; Mentz and Schiereck, 2008). Moeller and Schlingemann (2005) call this phenomenon the cross-border effect. The cross-border effect constitutes constantly smaller shareholder gains from international than domestic acquisitions due to the lower coordination efforts at domestic acquisitions. Concluding, the findings from the overall M&A research, horizontal acquisitions combined with a national focus usually generate the most valuable wealth impact for bidding firms.

Although most studies based on cross-industrial samples disregard industry-specific effects, these findings also hold true in such highly competitive industries as the construction industry.[4] In such industries, market horizontal acquisitions usually do not entail market dominating positions but still create wealth for the bidders and are superior to unrelated acquisitions. A prime example for this phenomenon is the construction sector in matured markets. Despite the low growth potential in matured markets, construction services cannot simply be transferred to fast-growing markets, except these markets are locally close to the home market (McGraw-Hill Construction, 2006; Rottke and Wernecke, 2002). As an alternative, construction firms intend to raise their size on the home market. Increased business size enables construction firms to bid for lucrative big-scale projects (Delaney and Wamuziri, 2004). Subsequently, Delaney and Wamuziri (2004) report in their M&A study on the English construction and construction material market M&A specific returns of 8.19% for the acquirers. Choi and Russel (2004) support these findings with their domestic M&A study on the American construction market. They report 2.41% M&A returns for the bidding companies. Rottke et al. (2009) detect in their globally focused study share-

4 I receive a concentration level of below 1% when applying the Herfindahl-Hirschmann-Index. The number of construction firms in the US in 2006, which amounted over 1.2mn, might serve as an example (McGraw-Hill Construction, 2006).

holder wealth effects of 1.91% for the bidding construction companies. The latter study distinguishes between the different strategic focuses of the acquisition. Similar to previous research, they find for horizontal acquisitions abnormal returns of 2.88%, while conglomerate acquisitions destroy corporate value of up to -2.47%. Likewise, the study underlines for the construction industry the overall tendency to prefer domestic in comparison to international acquisitions. Rottke et al. (2009) report negative or only small positive capital market reactions to the announcement of international acquisitions for the bidding construction firms. Domestic takeovers are positively rewarded, particularly in countries undergoing a real estate boom. Comparable to the cross-industrial evidence, the results only serve as an indication, because only about 55% of the horizontal and domestic takeovers illustrate indeed positive results. The remaining 45% of construction bidders suffer negative impacts on their shareholder value from horizontal and domestic acquisitions, implying an inferiority of this M&A strategy for those firms. In this study, I address the issue under which circumstances the horizontal and domestic acquisitions strategy becomes detrimental for the shareholders. I apply the case study methodology for analyzing this subject in order to receive a comprehensive overview of the details and structure of the takeovers and the management decisions behind the acquisitions, which caused the destruction of the corporate value.

A prime example for the negative wealth effects from horizontal and domestic acquisitions is the German Walter Bau AG[5], the formerly third biggest German construction company. Similar to the English and American industry, the German market belongs to the matured construction markets with a high fragmentation of 80,000 construction firms (Hauptverband der Deutschen Bauindustrie, 2002). However, different from several matured markets, the German construction market also reported severe shrinking construction volumes of € 54bn (21%) in the period from 1995 until 2004 (Statistisches Bundesamt, 2008). To overcome this challenge and to improve its status on the market, Walter Bau engaged in various horizontal acquisitions mainly in the German market and even increased its domestic business share from 75% in 1996 to 80% in 2004 (Walter Bau, 1997; Bundesanzeiger Jahresabschlüsse, 2006). The decision to focus on the German market was made in accordance with the major shareholder of Walter Bau, Ignaz Walter, who also was the CEO and later on the chairman of the supervisory board of Walter Bau.

According to the overall findings on M&A and to Anand (2005), who assumes benefits from the consolidation and the abandonment of excessive assets and resources from related acquisitions on declining markets, this strategic behavior should have created additional shareholder value. This assumption holds partly true for most Walter Bau acquisitions, as the Walter Bau share achieved

5 In the following, "Walter Bau" refers to the legal entity "Walter Bau AG".

positive abnormal returns around the M&A announcement. Contrarily, target shareholders lost from the acquisition overall. Hence, these acquisitions reversed the often-observed phenomenon that wealth is transferred from the acquiring to the target shareholders at M&A. In addition, by extending the observation period by a couple of days, at almost all observed acquisitions the positive returns vanished and results turned negative. All positive effects seem to result in vain, which is supported by the consistent negative long-term results. The low or negative performance measures in the years after the acquisitions stress that the expected synergies from the mergers were not yielded. Most units continued to generate losses resulting in the group's insolvency in 2005.

Only the Dyckerhoff Systems International (DSI) unit produced consistent and raising profits for the company. DSI provided equipment and highly advanced technology for international mining companies in North America as well as technical solutions for international complex infrastructure projects. Obviously, DSI can neither be regarded as a typical construction firm nor do they have their business focus on the German market. The 2004 earnings before interest and taxes (EBIT) of the HOCHTIEF AG[6], the biggest German construction firm, supports this finding. Almost 60% of the HOCHTIEF EBIT in 2004 came from the business in Asia and Australia (HOCHTIEF, 2005). Hence, I demonstrate within this study that under certain circumstances such as declining and fragmented markets, national acquisitions are inferior to international diversification. Due to the strong alignment of management and principals at Walter Bau, I can exclude corporate governance issues in the observed case.

The remainder of this study is structured as follows. First, I introduce Walter Bau, its operations as well as its economic development until its insolvency in 2005. Later, I illustrate the major acquired targets and the transaction motives behind these acquisitions. In respect to the acquisition announcements, I analyze the short-term capital market reactions and thus the wealth effects to the transaction announcements by Walter Bau by the means of the event study methodology. I also employ capital market performance measurement methods to examine the long-term wealth effects of those acquisitions for the shareholders. In the context of assessing the wealth effect of those transactions and the interdependency of the acquisitions to the insolvency, I also provide a survey about the influence of the examined M&A on Walter Bau's performance and liquidity measures. I conclude the findings by highlighting the crucial aspects of Walter Bau's M&A strategy, its impact on the company's successive destruction and the reasoning why national acquisitions in declining and competitive markets result in detrimental effects for the acquirer.

---

6 In the following, "HOCHTIEF" refers to the legal entity "HOCHTIEF AG"

4.2 Acquirer and Targets

4.2.1 The Acquirer Walter Bau

In 1962 Ignaz Walter established an engineering and architectural office and in the subsequent year the construction firm Universal-Bau Walter (UBW) GmbH in Augsburg, Germany. The principal business activities were architectural, engineering and building construction services. In 1978 Ignaz Walter acquired the Thosti AG, a construction firm that was founded in 1865 and thus accounted for the oldest of all Walter Bau units. Ignaz Walter himself became the CEO of the merged company, which remained with the headquarters in Augsburg (Gaertner and Seidel, 2005). In the following years, the business was continuously expanded by endogenous growth as well as further acquisitions of German construction firms. In 1991 the company is renamed to Walter Bau and its legal form is shifted to a public company (AG). In the period from the Thosti takeover until the IPO of the Walter Bau, on February 27, 1992, Walter Bau raised the turnover more than fourfold from € 187mn to € 1,408mn and the earnings from € 1mn to € 22mn. Additionally, Walter Bau enjoyed within those 14 years a constant cash inflow, which led to a cash stock of € 263mn after € 12mn in 1978. The earnings and cash development allowed Walter Bau to almost double the dividend payments to the shareholders. In equal measure, the staff increased from 3,670 to 10,962 employees. The equity-to-assets ratio amounted to 16.7% (Walter Bau, 1992). The initial price of the Walter Bau share was € 39.42 (Bloomberg, 2008; Walter Bau, 1992). The Walter Holding AG, which belonged to 100% to Ignaz Walter himself, held 75% of the common share and 64% of the total equity (common stock and preferred stock). Another 16.9% of the total equity belonged to the Federal Bank of Bavaria. The remaining shares were free-floating (Walter Bau, 1993; Börsen-Zeitung; 1999, Gaertner and Seidel, 2005).

Benefiting from the construction boom in Germany after the reunification, Walter Bau continued to grow in the following three years. The sales rose by 48% to € 2,090mn and the Cash and Equivalents by 25% to € 330. The equity-to-assets ratio even rose to 25%. This growth velocity also required new employees, entailing an additional 7% of staff by the end of 1995. In comparison to 1994, the staff was, however, reduced by 9%. Similarly, the earnings shrank to € 11mn, which was a reduction of -57% in 1994 and -50% to the year 1991. The capital market considered those decreases with a reduction of the share price by -59%.

By then the business of the Walter Bau had been strongly extended to various other fields in the construction sector. The company executed turnkey construction for any types of buildings such as residential premises, shopping malls and other sorts of non-residential buildings. Five years later, these works were enhanced by the introduction of an innovative procedure to set buildings more safely in not easily urbanized areas such as swampy grounds. Turnkey construction as the major business field of Walter Bau contributed 50% to the total sales. Another essential sector for Walter Bau was, with about 25%, the civil engineering sector. Within the context of civil engineering, Walter Bau built bridges, tunnels, sewage treatment plants and any type of industrial plants. With new developments such as the Match-Cast-Incremental launching method, where the superstructure of the bridge has different ground geometry than the foundations, it tried to actively strengthen its position in the construction market. Similar to other construction firms, Walter Bau also intended to find practicable solutions for new challenges. For example, in 1996 it developed new systems for sewage treatment plants, so that these plants could be more easily set up in densely urbanized areas. Next to civil engineering projects, Walter Bau operated in the traffic route engineering sector, which accounted for around 15% of the turnovers. Here, Walter Bau constructed highways, roads and streets as well as entire systems for airfields and rail tracks. The latter set high requirements on the used concrete for the tracks as the high-speed train ICE was launched in Germany in the mid-nineties. Walter Bau introduced a specific type of prestressed concrete that was impermeable and low in alkali. This constitution of the concrete assures a firm basement for railway tracks and permits trains to run speeds of up to 300 km/h (188 miles/h). Next to these pure construction activities, Walter Bau also continued to conduct planning, engineering and architectural services. Walter Bau even extended its services to related fields like project development and real estate operations. Furthermore, it provided final customers and other construction firms with the sale and delivery of construction materials, shipping services and the sale, renting and maintenance of construction machinery. The construction-related services contributed a minor share of 10%, or slightly less to the entire group turnover (Walter Bau, 1992–1999).

Figure 4.1: Organizational Structure of Walter Bau in 1995

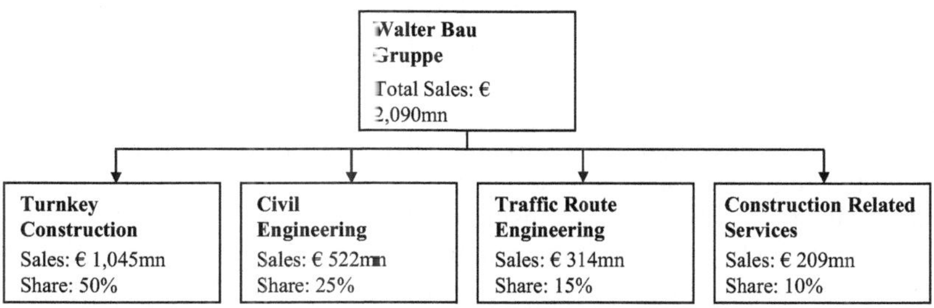

Figure 4.1 illustrates the upper level of the organizational structure of the Walter Bau, including the turnover of each unit and its share on the total turnover of the firm three years after the IPO (Walter Bau, 1993).

Even though it expanded its business to the different fields of the construction sector, the international business was of minor relevance before the acquisition of the Concrete Construction Group in 1996. As a consequence, the foreign activities were included within the four major business units. After the reunification construction boom in Germany during the first half of the nineties, the German construction market underwent one of its strongest recessions in the decade from 1995–2004. Based on the 1995 price level, the total construction expenditures decreased successively from € 258.8bn to € 204.6bn in Germany within this period (Statistisches Bundesamt, 2008). Obviously, this recession also hit the domestic-oriented Walter Bau. The board of Walter Bau recognized these potential challenges on the home market in the mid-nineties and decided to enlarge the geographical scale of the company's operations (Walter Bau, 1997).

Until the end of the millennium, Walter Bau extended foreign activities with the acquisition of the Australian Concrete Construction Group, thereby reaching to over 30% of total sales in 1999. Despite this increase of revenue streams and further sales growth by an annual average of 4.6% to an amount of € 2,484mn in 1999, the profitability of Walter Bau began to worsen. In 1997 the earnings amounted to a low positive result of € 3mn. Although the earnings revived slightly to € 5mn in the subsequent year, they again decreased to a value of € 3.3mn in 1999. The operating income even dropped below zero to € -46mn. Only by a withdrawal of € 52.3mn from the retained earnings and by the acceptance of a decline in the equity-to-assets ratio to 16% the positive result could be achieved (Walter Bau, 1997–2000). The liquidity remained almost on a constant level. However, significant parts of the liquidity were bound to bank guarantees and thus were not freely disposable. Corresponding to the declining profits, the share price fell to € 9. Owing to the negative operating profits, for the first time in the company's history, the earnings per share (EPS) turned negative to € -3.3 (Thomson Financial, 2009). The development of market-to-book value was even worse with a drop down to 0.3, inferring low growth expectations for the company. This tense financial situation required a layoff of 8% of the staff. In 1995, 11,736 people still worked for Walter Bau. In 1999, the number dropped to 10,811.

This negative trend continued during the first years of the new millennium, although the company intended to strengthen its market position in the German market with two big domestic acquisitions. With the acquisition of the Heilit Wörner AG in 2000, the sales of the combined enterprise peaked to over € 4bn. In comparison to the revenues of both companies on a stand-alone basis of € 3.6bn in 1999, the combined entity was able to boost the sales by 11%. Nevertheless, the relevance of the foreign activities plunged again from 31% to 21% due to this merger.

The integration of the DYWIDAG AG in 2001 did not have the same positive effect on revenues, as the revenues reduced by 2% to € 3.9bn (Walter Bau,

2000 and 2001). Still, in respect to the revenue measure, Walter Bau became the third biggest construction company in Germany behind the number one HOCHTIEF and the number two Bilfinger Berger AG[7]. Because of the high fragmentation of the German construction market with a total of 80,000 operating construction firms, the market share only rose from 1.3% to 1.5% (Hauptverband der Deutschen Bauindustrie, 2002; Walter Bau, 2002; Statistisches Bundesamt, 2008). In addition, the prices for construction services decreased by 30% since the mid-nineties because of the strong competition from foreign competitors, causing tightening profit margins for the entire German construction industry (Walter Bau, 2001 and 2002). Obviously, financial difficulties continued for the German construction firms, including Walter Bau. The operating profits of Walter Bau deteriorated in the following years. In 2000 the EBIT decreased to € -3mn and the net loss even reduced to € -64mn. In 2001, the situation became even more severe. The operating losses exceeded € -142mn and the total loss even € -230mn. The earnings per share declined to € -5, the lowest value in the company's history. Additionally, the liquidity of Walter Bau vanished within these years by 36% to € 256mn. This negative development created a severe drop of the equity-to-assets ratio to 11%, implying an exhaustion of the equity reserves (Walter Bau, 2002).

From this corrosion of the profits and the equity capital Walter Bau did not recover, even though Walter Bau restructured the organization of the company and provided more importance to profitable units, e.g., the DSI business. Walter Bau also stressed the relevance of the foreign business by summarizing most foreign construction activities into an organizationally separated business segment. Still, the foreign turnkey and civil engineering construction business remained on a low level of 16%, and by including the foreign traffic route works, the foreign sales amounted to around 20% (Walter Bau, 2002).

However, neither the acquisitions nor the restructuring of the business could prevent the further descent of Walter Bau. Although the EBIT turned positive again to € 4mn and € 15mn in 2002 and 2003 and the net income also depicted slight positive values of € 0.2mn and € 2mn respectively, the profitability of the original construction business did not return. The positive results mainly stemmed from extraordinary incomes, which were accomplished from the sale of assets of the acquired companies (Walter Bau, 2003 and 2004). In addition to the profitability decline, the customers ordered fewer projects from Walter Bau. The -24% cutback in the revenues from ca. € 4bn in 2000 to ca. € 3bn in 2003 was -11% worse than the general downturn of the German construction volume of -13%. This slump in revenues and profits entailed a discharge of 38% of all employees within the period 2001–2003 (Walter Bau, 2001 and 2004; Euroconstruct, 2004).

---

7 In the following "Bilfinger Berger" refers to "Bilfinger Berger AG"

Figure 4.2: Organizational Structure of Walter Bau in 2001

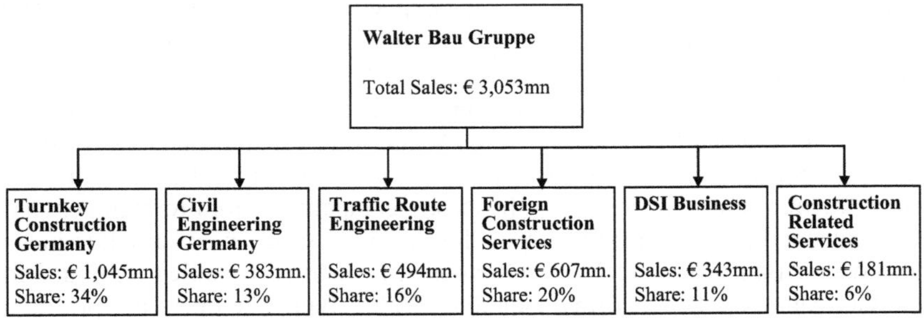

Figure 4.2 illustrates the upper level of the organizational structure of Walter Bau, including the turnover of each unit and its share on the total turnover of the firm after ca. 10 years of being listed in the CDAX (Walter Bau, 2002).

Despite these difficulties in October 2004, Walter Bau intended to purchase the fifth biggest construction firm on the German market, the Züblin AG. The take-over never occurred because the Federal Bank of Baden-Württemberg rejected the merger by not warranting the necessary guaranteed credits for Züblin in the case of the acquisition. Due to this development, several banks lost their confidence in the business and a turnaround of Walter Bau. The required prolongation of the guarantees was blocked for the Walter Bau construction projects by three banks in January 2005 (Handelsblatt, 2005a; Manager Magazin, 2005). Consequently, on February 1, 2005, Germany's third biggest construction company, Walter Bau, and most of the 59 agencies of the Walter Bau Group filed for insolvency (Financial Times Deutschland, 2005; Handelsblatt, 2005b).

Table 4.1: Historical Overview of Walter Bau

Year	Event
1962	Ignaz Walter establishes an engineering and architectural office in Augsburg, Germany
1963	Ignaz Walter establishes the construction firm Universal-Bau Walter GmbH (UBW) GmbH
1978	Acquisition of the construction firm Thosti AG; Ignaz Walter becomes CEO
1983	Universal-Bau Walter acquires the construction firm Boswau + Knauer AG; Universal-Bau Walter GmbH, Thosti AG and Boswau + Knauer AG merge to WTB (Walter-Thosti-Boswau)
1986	Ignaz Walter purchases the majority stake of 75.2% in the Heilit Woerner AG; Ignaz Walter becomes the chairman of the supervisory board of the Heilit Woerner AG

1988 WTB acquires the majority stake of 53.6% in the Züblin AG; Ignaz Walter becomes the chairman of the supervisory board of Züblin AG

1991 WTB is transformed into Walter Bau AG

1992 IPO of Walter Bau AG; 1.5mn shares were issued at a price of € 39.42

1992 Ignaz Walter purchases the majority stake of 76% in the Dyckerhoff & Widmann AG (DYWIDAG); Ignaz Walter becomes the chairman of the supervisory board of DYWIDAG

1994 Ignaz Walter transfers the majority stakes in the Heilit Wörner AG and DYWIDAG into the Walter Holding AG

1996 Walter Bau AG acquires the Australian Concrete Constructions Group for € 25mn; Ignaz Walter resigns as CEO of the Walter Bau AG and becomes the chairman of the supervisory board of the Walter Bau AG; liquid funds peak to € 520mn

1999 First net losses at the Walter Bau AG of € -49mn

2000 Merger of Walter Bau AG and Heilit Wörner AG; Terms of conditions are 7 Walter Bau AG shares for 10 Heilit Wörner AG shares and a cash payment of € 0.02 for each ordinary share as well as € 0.07 for each preferred share; net loss raises to € -65mn

2001 Walter Bau AG acquires DYWIDAG for € 81mn. Terms of conditions are 9 new ordinary shares for 10 DYWIDAG shares, plus € 0.03 in cash for every DYWIDAG share; Walter Bau sells 4.9% of its Züblin stake; net losses of € -253mn; liquid funds drop to € 256mn

2002 Divesture of the 48.7% stake in Züblin planned; Net income of € 0.26mn

2003 Construction business remains unprofitable; Net income of € 2mn results from divesture of assets of € 41.8mn

2004 Ignaz Walter tries to merge the Walter Bau AG with the Züblin AG; the planned merger is averted by the Federal Bank of BadenWürttemberg; liquid funds decrease to € 126 mn

2005 Banks reject further bank guarantees to the Walter Bau AG; in February the Walter Bau AG and most of its 59 units file for insolvency

Table 4.1 provides an overview about the beginning, the ascendancy and the descent of Walter Bau. It focuses mainly on the acquisitions by the Walter Bau AG as well as the cross-ownership of Ignaz Walter. The documented net income/loss and financial funds numbers illustrate the difficult situation Walter Bau had faced since the late nineties.

Table 4.2: Walter Bau in Numbers

Year	1991	1992	1993	1994	1995	1996	1997	1998	1999	2000	2001	2002	2003	2004
Total Sales (in € mn.)	1,408	1,767	1,871	1,999	2,090	2,325	2,517	2,398	2,484	4,013	3,923	3,325	3,053	2,779
Share of Foreign Sales	7.3%	7.7%	10.2%	9.9%	9.8%	21.9%	24.7%	32.2%	31.6%	20.7%	15.6%	19.1%	19.9%	19.8%
EBIT (in € mn.)	38	39	42	38	13	3	8	9	(42)	(3)	(142)	4	15	(192)
Net Income/Loss (in € mn.)	22	20	25	26	11	2	3	5	(46)	(65)	(231)	-	2	(1,579)
Cash Equivalents (in € mn.)	263	370	298	283	330	529	467	423	403	435	256	232	222	42
Total Assets (in € mn.)	720	973	938	941	1,057	1,382	1,290	1,265	1,272	1,864	1,610	1,504	1,393	1,873
Equity/Total Assets	16.7%	22.1%	25.2%	26.9%	25.3%	18.6%	19.8%	19.7%	15.8%	16.1%	10.9%	10.5%	10.7%	-72.4%
Net Profit Margin	1.6%	1.1%	1.3%	1.3%	0.5%	0.1%	0.1%	0.2%	-1.9%	-1.6%	-5.9%	0.0%	0.1%	-56.8%
Return on Equity (ROE)	18.6%	9.2%	10.4%	10.3%	4.2%	0.6%	1.2%	2.0%	-23.1%	-21.6%	-131.8%	0.2%	1.4%	n.a.
Return on Capital Employed (ROCE)	15.9%	8.0%	8.2%	6.5%	2.0%	0.5%	1.1%	1.3%	-6.4%	-0.3%	-15.8%	0.5%	2.3%	-18.3%
Earnings per Share (EPS)	1.49	1.32	1.21	1.35	1.48	0.47	0.20	0.33	-3.30	-2.63	-5.00	-0.01	0.03	n.a.
Current Ratio	1.18	1.49	1.60	1.90	2.00	1.59	1.65	1.61	1.58	1.79	1.53	1.49	1.33	0.22
Quick Ratio	0.84	1.24	1.25	1.51	1.69	1.31	1.36	1.33	1.29	1.44	1.19	1.24	1.15	0.21
Cash Ratio	0.55	0.77	0.70	0.81	0.85	0.80	0.80	0.71	0.65	0.53	0.36	0.33	0.30	0.05
Employees	10,962	12,560	12,489	12,839	11,736	12,550	11,579	10,521	10,811	16,502	14,472	11,516	10,143	4,169

Table 4.2 illustrates the yearly development of selected accounting numbers, performance and liquidity indicators and staff of the Walter Bau AG over the horizon 1991 – 2004. Accounting numbers are illustrated in million euros and performance as well as liquidity indicators either as percentage- or non-percentage ratios. The Employee number comprises all clerks and industrial workers employed at the Walter Bau AG (Bundesanzeiger Jahresabschlüsse, 2006; ThomsonFinancials, 2009; Walter Bau, 1992 – 2004).

4.2.2 Target 1: Concrete Construction Group

Walter Bau's biggest foreign investment was the acquisition of Concrete Construction Group in Sydney, Australia in 1996 (Walter Bau, 1997). Before the acquisition, the Concrete Construction Group was held by three private investors (73%) and their employees (23%). With the transaction, Walter Bau pursued the opportunity to grow in the attractive Asian and Australian market. The Olympic Games in Sydney 2000 caused a construction boom in the country. Several East Asian countries also experienced high growth rates. In particular, China underwent a decade with double-digit growth rates. In the second half of the nineties, China's construction market grew on average by 11% and, in the first years of the new millennium, by more than 20% (National Bureau of Statistics China, 2006). The Concrete Construction Group was able to participate in those construction volume upswings, which showed immediate effects on the revenues of Walter Bau. Within the year of the acquisition, the foreign revenues more than doubled to an amount of € 505mn. Nevertheless, Walter Bau even expected higher revenues from the Australian acquisition, but all unprofitable acquisitions were abandoned, thereby reducing the expected revenue contribution by € 100mn. Although this value was still below Walter Bau's expectation, the turnover rose to € 600mn. The foundation for the extension of foreign business activities seemed to be set (Walter Bau, 1997).

4.2.3 Target 2: Heilit Wörner

The Heilit Wörner AG roots reach back to the year 1871, when Mr. Heilmann started a construction business in Bavaria, Germany, which eventually became the Heilmann and Littmann GmbH. Over the years the legal form shifted, and the structure of the owners changed. In 1980 the company was merged with the construction firm Sager and Wörner into Heilit Wörner AG.[8] In 1986 Ignaz Walter acquired the majority stake of 75% in Heilit Wörner. Eight years later Ignaz Walter transferred this stake into the Walter Bau Holding AG[9], which he and his family owned to 100% (Börsen-Zeitung, 1999; Gaertner and Seidel, 2005). Heilit Wörner provided services in most fields of the construction sector, where construction of residential and non-residential buildings represented the major part of the revenues. Around 46% of the revenues of € 1,118mn stemmed from this section in 1999. The civil engineering projects accounted for 24%, road and other type of asphalt construction for 25% and miscellaneous construction related services for 5% (Heilit Wörner, 2000).

---

8 In the following, "Heilit Wörner" refers to the legal entity "Heilit Wörner AG".

9 In the following "Walter Bau Holding" refers to the legal entity "Walter Bau Holding AG"

The main rationale of the acquisition, however, was the integration of the lucrative road and asphalt construction unit of Heilit Wörner. The company was particularly famous and well recognized for its advanced technology in the construction of roads, airport runways and other asphalt surfaces. The applied technology enhances the time of usage of any concrete or asphalt surfaces and allows the transport of heavy carriers without suffering damage to the lanes. With this new technology, Heilit Wörner competed for road construction contracts in the German market and also in other European markets. For instance, in 1999, Heilit Wörner built several highways in Poland and was responsible for the compilation of the airfield for freight carriage on the international airport in Paris, France. Other units also operated on an international scale, as for example the civil engineering unit with the construction of large-sized water treatment facilities (Heilit Wörner, 2000).

With a share of 83%, the majority of the revenues came from the construction activities in Germany. During the nineties, the construction volume in Germany increased even by 16% while the foreign activities decreased by -10%. The negative development of foreign projects, mainly due to difficulties in Canada, caused this decline. However, Heilit Wörner still achieved a total construction volume increase of 10% in 1999, but, like other German construction firms, faced strong competition in the declining German market. The operations led to a negative EBIT of € -7.6mn. In the years before, the EBIT showed positive figures between € 6.4mn and € 13.3mn. The same accounted for the net income numbers. While from 1995–1998 the net income amounted to values between €1.6mn and € 7.7mn, in 1999 the income turned into a loss of € -9.3mn. Hence, both Walter Bau as well as Heilit Wörner started into the merger with a combined operating loss of almost € -60mn (Heilit Wörner, 2000; Walter Bau, 2000).

4.2.4 Target 3: DYWIDAG

The history of the DYWIDAG AG (Dyckerhoff und Widmann AG)[10] traces back to the year 1865, when Heinrich Land and Wilhelm Dyckerhoff founded the Lang and Cie concrete factory. In 1867 Gottlieb Widmann joined the associates of the company and Lang and Cie was changed to Dyckerhoff und Widmann (DYWIDAG, 2009). In 1991 Ignaz Walter purchased 51% of the DYWIDAG shares. In 1992 he increased the share to 76% and in 1994 finally transferred this majority stake to the Walter Bau Holding (Börsen-Zeitung, 1999; Gaertner and Seidel, 2005).

DYWIDAG focused mainly on general construction services in the construction building and civil engineering sector. This business included the resi-

10 In the following, "DYWIDAG" refers to the legal entity "DYWIDAG AG".

dential and non-residential construction business as well as the civil engineering sector, in particular the planning and erecting of industrial plants. The shares on the company turnover were unequally distributed. While the building construction represented around 75%, the civil engineering only contributed 8% to total sales in 2000. Another 4% resulted from the production of precast concrete elements and the compilation of these elements into construction systems. These systems, for example, are used for staircases in stadiums. Next to the construction-related activities, 10% of the revenues were generated by the DYWIDAG Systems International (DSI) unit. This unit mainly worked internationally and provided engineering services for challenging and complex construction projects as well as mining operations. In addition to these services, they also engineered highly advanced technology products and systems for geo-engineering, mining and civil engineering. Any other engineering, planning or construction services were comprised within the remaining 3% of the business volume (DYWIDAG, 2001).

Although DYWIDAG had subsidiaries in all continents, around 85% of the business was generated in the German market. The construction building unit was the biggest segment within the firm. This unit exclusively concentrated on the domestic market. This explains the predominance in the German business. Due to this strong domestic focus, DYWIDAG was also hit by the recession of the German construction market. Even though in the beginning of the recession, the revenues were raised by 30% to € 2,155mn in 1997 but declined by almost 38% afterwards until the merger with Walter Bau in 2001. Likewise, the performance decreased drastically from an EBIT value of € 28mn and a net income of € 21mn in 1996 to an EBIT of € -25mn and a respective net loss of € -34mn in 2000. Losses from the German building construction caused this negative profit development. The only consistently profitable division remained the international DSI business with an average EBIT of € 7mn (DYWIDAG, 1997–2001; Thomson Financial, 2009). Like the situation of the Heilit Wörner transaction, both parties reported negative results before the merger. But with the integration of DYWIDAG into Walter Bau, the top-management assessed the merger as an unique opportunity to redeploy their resources efficiently in order to cut costs, to increase the competitiveness and market power as well as to return to a positive operating performance (Börsen-Zeitung, 2001a; Manager Magazin, 2001; Walter Bau, 2001).

4.2.5 Target 4: Züblin

The Züblin AG was founded by Eduard Züblin as a concrete and iron construction company in Strasbourg, France, in 1898. The expansion of the company occurred rapidly. Within the subsequent years, the company set up various subsidiaries all over Europe. After the First World War and the death of Eduard

Züblin in 1916, the German subsidiary in Stuttgart continued the construction operations as Züblin AG (Züblin, 2009)[11].

Züblin was involved in all relevant fields of the construction industry like building construction, civil engineering and any infrastructure works as well as construction engineering. Züblin also operated production factories for precast concrete elements. In addition, Züblin tried to support and enhance all of its construction operations by a competence center specializing in advanced construction techniques and efficient conduction of construction projects. Despite the declining construction volumes on the German market, Züblin maintained its turnover at a constant level between 2000 and 2004, although around 80% of the business concentrated on the German market. The company also reported persistently positive EBIT values between € 3mn and € 20mn even in the most severe recession years 2001 and 2002. The positive operating earnings usually entailed net incomes. Nevertheless, in 2001 and 2003, the company suffered a net loss of € -25mn and € -5mn. The negative effects were mainly caused by extraordinary expenses from turnkey construction projects. Hence, the steadily raising competition in the construction building sector also partly affected Züblin, especially as this unit accounted for ca. 50% of the entire revenues. Nonetheless, the engineering services, facility management service as well as the project development department contributed stable earnings, which mostly offset losses from the building construction sector. Finally, the precast concrete factories reported small revenues, implying minor influence of these units on the entire business of Züblin. (Züblin, 2001–2005).

The motive of the planned acquisition of Züblin was ambiguous. Walter Bau itself stressed, on the one hand, the rising market power on the domestic market. On the other hand, Walter Bau evaluated Züblin's activities and geographical focus as complementary to its own business (Handelsblatt, 2004). On the contrary, there were assumptions Walter Bau intended to abuse the acquisition for the rehabilitation of its unstable financial conglomerate (Seidel, 2004). The ownership structure might support this assumption. Walter Bau did not have to expect a strong resistance to this acquisition, as it already owned a stake of 48.7% in the Züblin. The other major stakeholder, the Lenz family, was willing to sell its 43% stake to Walter Bau. As aforementioned, the Federal Bank of Baden-Württemberg opposed and prevented the acquisition (Handelsblatt, 2005a; Manager Magazin, 2005).

Concluding, Walter Bau was already interwoven with all domestic targets before the acquisitions. Although Walter Bau, Heilit Wörner and DYWIDAG operated independently and did not possess financial stakes in one another, the three companies were interwoven through the Walter Bau Holding, which controlled all three firms. Although, Züblin is not directly controlled by the Walter

---

11 In the following, "Züblin" refers to the legal entity "Züblin AG".

Bau Holding, Ignaz Walter also has major influence on Züblin through the stake of Walter Bau in Züblin. Obviously, Ignaz Walter and not the management of the involved firms eventually decided about the acquisition of the domestic targets and their integration into Walter Bau. Subsequently, the owner of the acquirer and the domestic targets seemed to expect further positive impacts from the strategy to concentrate the construction business on the German market.

4.3 Methodology

4.3.1 Methodology for the Short-Term Analysis

I apply the event study methodology regarding Brown and Warner (1985) for detecting the short-term wealth effects on Walter Bau due to its acquisitions announcements.

$$AR_{w,t} = R_{w,t} - \overline{R}_{w,t}$$

$AR_{w,t}$ refers to the abnormal return of the Walter Bau share after the acquisition announcement. The abnormal return is calculated by subtracting the estimated share returns $\overline{R}_{w,t}$ of the Walter Bau share from its actual returns $R_{w,t}$. The estimated returns are calculated by the market model formula:

$$\overline{R}_{w,t} = \overline{\alpha}_w + \overline{\beta}_w * \overline{R}_{m,t}$$

$\overline{R}_{w,t}$ depicts the expected return of the Walter Bau share. $\overline{R}_{m,t}$ describes the return of the selected reference index. To receive a detailed picture about the performance, I use the leading German index CDAX and the world construction index within the analysis. The variable $\overline{\alpha}_w$ represents the market independent part and $\overline{\beta}_w$ the impact of the market return on Walter Bau's share return. The estimation period comprises 252 trading days before the event window. After calculating the abnormal returns, the daily abnormal returns are added up to the cumulated abnormal returns (CAR):

$$CAR_{w,[t,T]} = \sum_{t=1}^{T} AR_{w,t}$$

As I observe the wealth effects on the acquisition announcement I consider the CAR values for Walter Bau and the targets and the combined entity provided that data for the target is available. To calculate the CAR values of the combined entity $CAR_{c,t}$ I weigh the CAR values of Walter Bau and the target company according to their market values one day before the transaction (Bradley et al., 1988):

$$CAR_{c,[t,T]} = \frac{CAR_{w,[t,T]} * MV_w + CAR_{i,[t,T]} * MV_i}{MV_w + MV_i}$$

4.3.2 Methodology for the Long-Term Analysis

For the investigation of the long-term performance, I apply the buy-and-hold abnormal return (BHAR) approach regarding Lvon et al. (1999). In the analysis, I compare the buy-and-hold returns of Walter Bau to the indices CDAX and the world construction index as well as to a reference portfolio consisting of the major German competitors of Walter Bau.

$$BHAR_{w,[t,T]} = \prod_{t=1}^{T}(1+R_{w,t}) - \prod_{t=1}^{T}(1+R_{j,t})$$

The cumulated product of $(1+R_{w,t})$ defines the buy-and-hold return of Walter Bau over the time interval from t until T. The cumulated product of $(1+R_{j,t})$ defines the buy-and-hold return of the reference portfolio over the time interval from t until T. By subtracting the buy-and-hold returns of the reference index or reference portfolio from the buy-and-hold returns of Walter Bau, I obtain the buy-and-hold abnormal return for Walter for the T-months period.

4.4 Analysis of the M&A strategy of Walter Bau

After more than 30 years of operations in the field of turnkey construction, geotechnics, construction engineering, infrastructure technique and project development, declining turnovers as well as the tense profit and liquidity situation forced Walter Bau to terminate its business in 2005. The liquidator of Walter Bau declared the company's strategy to concentrate its business on the home market in spite of the enduring recession on the German construction market as one major reason for the corporate failure (Bundesanzeiger Jahresabschlüsse, 2008). In the following chapter, I investigate whether this strategy including the strong domestic focus of most acquisitions, influenced the corporate difficulties and finally its failure.

As aforementioned from 1995–2004 the German construction market had undergone a decade of declining construction volumes. This negative development severely influenced the market valuation of Walter Bau. The share price fell as low as € 2.15 until the end of 2004, inferring a shareholder wealth destruction of 95% within ca. 13 years after the IPO. Certainly, this recession also affected the competitors, but in comparison to Walter Bau, the biggest German construction company HOCHTIEF lost only -57% and the number two Bilfinger Berger -36% within the same period. In addition, from 2003 on, the share price of the two leading construction firms began to rise again, while the Walter Bau share remained on the bottom (Bloomberg, 2008).

Figure 4.3: Share Prices of Leading Construction Firms in Germany

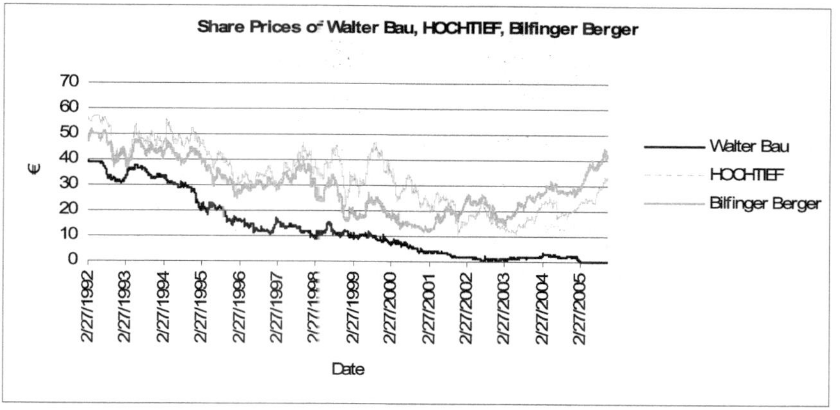

Figure 4.3 compares the share price devolution of the three biggest German construction firms HOCHTIEF, Bilfinger Berger and Walter Bau from 1992 until 2005, when Walter Bau filed for insolvency (Bloomberg, 2008).

This dispersion of the share price development is closely aligned to the different strategies of HOCHTIEF and Bilfinger Berger on the one hand and Walter Bau on the other. Until the early nineties, HOCHTIEF and Bilfinger Berger focused, similar to Walter Bau, their activities on the German construction market (Bilfinger Berger, 2009; HOCHTIEF, 2009). Since then HOCHTIEF and Bilfinger Berger drastically changed their business focus and vehemently pursued an international growth strategy by distributing their business to various countries. In 2004 nearly 70% of the total turnover of Bilfinger Berger came from international activities and at HOCHTIEF even more than 80%. In addition, the companies extended their business fields towards construction-related businesses, e.g., the operations of airports and power and industry plants. They also provided high advanced technical construction knowledge as well as facility management to their customers. The exploitations of new business fields allowed both firms to distribute their revenue streams and to become more independent from the declining and highly competitive German construction market. Not surprisingly, the development and operation services at HOCHTIEF contributed with 15% the same share to the company's earnings before taxes (EBT) like the original construction business did in Europe in 2004 (Bilfinger Berger, 2005; HOCHTIEF, 2005). Walter Bau also announced in 1996 to increase the foreign share to over 50% in the near future. With the acquisition of the Australian Concrete Construction Group, Walter Bau indeed seemed to follow this strategy, but a couple of years later the strategy was reversed and the foreign share dropped even below its value in 1996.

4.4.1 The Acquisition of Concrete Construction Group

On May 10, 1995, Walter Bau announced to acquire the Australian Concrete Construction Group. In 1996 the acquisition was executed for a price of ca. € 25mn. At first glance, the capital market rewarded the intention of Walter Bau to diversify its business internationally. Whether the German leading index CDAX or the Construction World index served as the reference index, the CAR values showed a positive wealth effect of up to 4.08% for Walter Bau. Nevertheless, with a prolongation of the observation period, the positive abnormal returns turned into strong wealth losses of up to -11%. It seems as if the capital market assumed financial burdens for Walter Bau from economic difficulties of the Concrete Construction Group.

Table 4.3: Acquisition of Concrete Construction Group – CAR Values

Event Window	**[-20,+20]**	**[-10,+10]**	**[-5,+5]**	**[-3,3]**	**[-1,+1]**
CAR values of Walter Bau					
Ref.Ind.: CDAX	-11.07%	-5.48%	-0.14%	2.21%	4.08%
Ref.Ind.: Con. World	-10.66%	-5.95%	-0.35%	1.91%	3.58%

Table 4.3 illustrates the CAR values of Walter Bau at the acquisition announcement of the Australian Concrete Construction Group. In the results in the upper row, I apply the German leading index CDAX as the reference index. In the results in the lower row, I apply the World Construction index as the reference index.

These negative findings turned into facts in the subsequent years of the transaction. Although the Australian agency contributed a large amount to the foreign turnover of Walter Bau and was mainly responsible for the steep increase in foreign sales of 63% in the period 1996 to 2000, the acquisition caused financial burdens for Walter Bau rather than contributing a value-generating impact for the firm (Walter Bau, 1997–2004). The extensive aid payments from the headquarters to the subsidiary also affected the long-run performance of the Walter Bau share negatively.

In comparison to the German leading index CDAX, Walter Bau performed decreasingly lower after the acquisition. While in the first three months, the Walter Bau share just deviated by 20% from the CDAX; after 36 months the difference out passed the 90% mark. On the one hand, the dispersion of the overall German economy and the German construction sector might have been responsible for that development. In contrast to the construction sector, most German CDAX companies benefited from the upswing and the new economy boom in the second half of the nineties (Euroconstruct, 2001). On the other hand, Walter Bau also underperformed to its international as well as domestic competitors, even though in the first 6 months after the takeover the performance of Walter Bau slightly outperformed the domestic competitors. The international diversification strategy of the domestic competitors seemed to be more successful than the foreign M&A strategy of Walter Bau. Shedding light on the performance development of the Australian subsidiary supports this assumption.

Table 4.4: Acquisition of Concrete Construction Group – BHAR Values

Event Window	36 Months	24 Months	12 Months	6 Months	3 Months
BHAR Walter Bau to Indices					
Ref.Ind.: CDAX	-93.11%	-78.50%	-43.86%	-25.25%	-18.50%
Ref.Ind.: Con. World	-29.37%	-39.92%	-36.50%	-23.95%	-18.31%
BHAR of Walter Bau to Reference Firms					
Mean	-9.69%	-20.27%	-14.85%	0.93%	-2.42%
Median	-13.05%	-38.51%	-33.04%	-5.94%	-4.26%

Table 4.4 illustrates the BHAR values of Walter Bau after the acquisition of the Australian Concrete Construction Group. In the results in the two upper rows, I compare the buy and hold returns of Walter Bau with those of the German leading index CDAX and the World Construction index. In the lower two rows, I compare the buy and hold returns of Walter Bau with big German competitors.

Within the 12 months after the acquisition, the revenues reached far lower values than expected by Walter Bau. Projects with a total volume of € 100mn are abandoned due to their predicted unprofitability. In addition, the transaction led to a duplication of the conglomerate's liabilities, as the Concrete Construction Group operated a € 100mn hotel, which was completely debt financed (Süddeutsche Zeitung, 1997). Due to losses from a lawsuit, the Australian subsidiary reported a slight loss in the first year of its corporate affiliation (Walter Bau, 1997). In the following years, the performance picture of the subsidiary remained mixed. In 1997 the activities led to a profit, but the subsequent year the results turned negative again due to a reevaluation of the operated hotel (Walter Bau, 1998 and 1999). Afterward the performance suffered consistently from project amendments and legal difficulties from the period before the acquisition. (Walter Bau, 2001). Combined with the lower growth rates in the Australian construction sector after the Olympics in Sydney in 2000, the agency acquired far fewer new projects, reported declining revenues from its hotel operations and became even more unprofitable. Consequently, the subsidiary found itself in financial distress in 2001. It had to be restructured by an amount of ca. € 27mn (Walter Bau, 2002). The restructuring costs nearly amounted to the acquisition price and imply substantial difficulties in the subsidiary. Furthermore, Walter Bau had to pay the acquisition and restructuring expenditures but also had unforeseen difficulties at several construction projects at the Australian agency. Due to these persistent problems, the Walter Bau headquarters considered a sale of the Australian agency in 2002 but discarded this option as they predicted promising growth rates in the Australian construction sector (Walter Bau, 2002 and 2003). In contrast, Walter Bau engaged in further restructuring programs with a volume of € 5.09mn in order to increase the competitiveness in Australia. Despite these restructuring measures, the Australian subsidiary continued to sustain heavy losses in 2003 (Walter Bau, 2004).

These negative results surprise on the first glance, because the successful international acquisitions of HOCHTIEF and Bilfinger Berger imply benefits for German construction firms from geographical diversification. Nevertheless, the performance losses due to the acquisition of the Concrete Construction Group stemmed mostly from difficulties within the Concrete Construction Group prior to the acquisition. Hence, the question arises whether that particular acquisition in Australia accounts for the first step of an insufficient M&A strategy or if the general reported superiority of domestic acquisitions by Mentz and Schiereck (2008) as well as Moeller and Schlingemann (2005) also apply to Walter Bau. Therefore, I concentrate in the following analysis on the wealth effects resulting from the two major domestic acquisitions of Walter Bau.

4.4.2 The Acquisition of Heilit Wörner

The value of the Heilit Wörner transaction corresponded to € 15.2mn. The payment consisted mainly of a share swap. The Heilit Wörner shareholders received 7 Walter Bau shares for 10 Heilit Wörner shares. The Walter Bau share was valued at € 7.2 and the Heilit Wörner share at € 5.04. In addition, Walter Bau paid for € 0.02 for each ordinary share and € 0.07 for preferred share (Börsen-Zeitung, 2000a). The involved parties expected cost synergies from € 40mn annually (Walter Bau, 2000). These should have been achieved from the reduction of agencies, a consolidated bid management and layoffs of redundant employees (Frankfurter Allgemeine Zeitung, 1999). In the following years, 2,486 employees were discharged due to the shutdown of Heilit Wörner's building construction unit after the takeover. Before the acquisition, in both companies, the number of employees totaled 18,988 people and afterwards only 16,502 (Heilit Wörner, 2000; Walter Bau, 2000 and 2001). The capital market assessed the expected benefits differently and showed mixed reactions to the acquisition announcement.

While Walter Bau gained positive abnormal returns from the acquisition, the target suffered substantial losses from the acquisition announcement. Hence, the disciplinary effect of acquisitions described by the agency theory is turned upside down in the observed case. Jensen (1986) as well as Gosh and Lee (2000) refer to the disciplinary effect as the transmission of the good management performance of the acquirer to the bad management performance of the target company. Thereof, the target achieves high abnormal returns around the announcement date of its acquisition. In the observed case, the opposite occurred, inferring a transfer of good management performance from the target to the acquirer.

Table 4.5: Acquisition of Heilit Wörner – CAR Values

Event Window	[-20,+20]	[-10,+10]	[-5,+5]	[-3,3]	[-1,+1]
CAR values of Walter Bau					
Ref.Ind.: CDAX	-3.28%	7.15%	5.74%	1.84%	1.79%
Ref.Ind.: Con. World	-2.37%	7.94%	6.17%	1.77%	1.72%
CAR values of Heilit Woerner					
Ref.Ind.: CDAX	-21.24%	-14.17%	-24.69%	-7.28%	-2.31%
Ref.Ind.: Con. World	-21.30%	-14.34%	-24.69%	-7.28%	-2.40%
CAR values of Walter Bau & Heilit Woerner combined					
Ref.Ind.: CDAX	-5.63%	3.94%	0.93%	0.36%	1.08%
Ref.Ind.: Con. World	-4.85%	4.58%	1.29%	0.30%	1.01%

Table 4.5 illustrates the CAR values of Walter Bau, Heilit Wörner and the combined entity at the acquisition announcement of the German Heilit Wörner. In the results in the upper rows of each observation entity, I apply the German leading index CDAX as the reference index. In the results in the lower rows, I apply the World Construction index as the reference index.

The earnings per share performance of both companies confirm this assumption. Heilit Wörner's EPS-ratio persistently outperformed the one of Walter Bau. In 1995 and 1996, Heilit Wörner achieved higher EPS-ratios of 47% and 34% respectively. In the following years until the takeover, the differences even increased to more than 200%. Although Heilit Wörner suffered a net loss the year before its acquisition, Walter Bau even reported net losses fivefold bigger than Heilit Wörner (Walter Bau, 2000; Heilit Wörner, 2000). Due to these performance differences, Heilit Wörner minor shareholders did not accept the compensation payment for their shares and claimed a fair cash payment for the Heilit Wörner shares. Even though Walter Bau had sufficient liquid funds at this time, they rejected this request (Börsen-Zeitung, 2000a). Thus, it seems as if the acquisition did not only serve for strengthening competitiveness of Walter Bau in the road and asphalt construction sector but also added wealth from the target into the combined conglomerate. This finding holds true according to the depicted positive abnormal returns for the combined firm. However, the largest analyzed event window of 41 days implies negative wealth effects for the combined firm as well as Walter Bau itself. The long-term BHAR analysis affirms this negative implication.

While the long-term under performance against the German CDAX oscillated between -30% and -50%, the performance against the world construction index constantly worsened over the time horizon. This consistent dispersion between the Walter Bau share performance and the world construction index of up to -73% was worse than at the international acquisition of the Australian subsidiary. In addition, these differences indicate increasing growth rates of the construction sector in other regions of the world. Consequently, Walter Bau continued to suffer from the declining domestic revenues and profit margins, regardless of the enhancement in the road and asphalt construction business by the national horizontal acquisition. Although, Heilit Wörner achieved stable revenues of € 450mn–€ 500mn and contributed positive EBITs as well as net incomes between € 5mn and € 10mn in the subsequent years, the integration and restructuring costs more than offset the benefits (Walter Bau, 2000 and 2001).

Table 4.6: Acquisition of Heilit Wörner – BHAR Values

Event Window	36 Months	24 Months	12 Months	6 Months	3 Months
BHAR of Walter Bau to Indices					
Ref.Ind.: CDAX	-35.53%	-46.86%	-48.45%	-29.78%	-37.53%
Ref.Ind.: Con. World	-73.49%	-63.86%	-49.60%	-13.78%	-5.72%
BHAR of Walter Bau to Reference Firms					
Mean	-51.19%	-50.16%	-23.11%	-7.48%	8.11%
Median	-32.49%	-34.68%	-23.44%	-5.75%	9.02%

Table 4.6 illustrates the BHAR values of Walter Bau after the acquisition of Heilit Wörner. In the results in the first two rows I compare the buy and hold returns of Walter Bau with those of the German leading index CDAX and the World Construction index. In the third and fourth rows, I compare the buy and hold returns of Walter Bau with big German competitors.

Not surprisingly, the international highly diversified German construction firms in the benchmark portfolio documented a better performance than Walter Bau in nearly all event windows. There was a big difference between the first and second year. While in the first 12 months after the acquisition the performance of Walter Bau was -23% worse than the benchmark firms, the subsequent year the difference widened to -50% and remained on this level afterwards. This negative development in the 24- and 36-months observation may not only have resulted from the Heilit Wörner acquisition, but also from the second domestic acquisition of DYWIDAG in 2001.

4.4.3 The Acquisition of DYWIDAG

Ignaz Walter refused a potential merger between Walter Bau and DYWIDAG in 1999 due to the different structures of the companies, but in 2000 Walter Bau declared DYWIDAG as an optimal partner that complemented the Walter Bau business. Thus Walter Bau decided to purchase DYWIDAG completely (Frankfurter Allgemeine Zeitung, 1999; Börsen-Zeitung, 2000b). In 2001 DYWIDAG was fully integrated into the Walter Bau conglomerate. Likewise to the Heilit Wörner takeovers, the DYWIDAG transaction was financed by a share swap with a combined small cash payment for each DYWIDAG share. For 10 DYWIDAG shares, the shareholders received 9 Walter Bau shares. The additional cash payment amounted to € 0.03 per share (Börsen-Zeitung, 2001). In total the transaction was valued at almost € 81mn (Thomson Financial, 2009). The exchange rate of shares implied a similar corporate value of both firms even though Walter Bau reported twice as big a turnover as DYWIDAG. Hence, DYWIDAG seemed to be more profitable than Walter Bau. By comparing the

EPS-ratios of the two firms, this assumption can be affirmed. The EPS-ratio of DYWIDAG was more than twofold higher than this of Walter Bau. In addition, DYWIDAG possessed valuable asstes of € 255mn (Koehn, 2001). Several insiders assumed that Walter Bau would use the transaction to rehabilitate its profitability and liquidity situation, mainly by selling the premises after the transaction (Börsen-Zeitung, 2001a; Koehn and Bein, 2001; Manager Magazin, 2001). Although Ignaz Walter contradicted this assumption (Süddeutsche Zeitung, 2004), the CAR values around the acquisition announcement support this thesis.

Table 4.7: Acquisition of DYWIDAG – CAR Values

Event Window	[-20,+20]	[-10,+10]	[-5,+5]	[-3,3]	[-1,+1]
CAR values of Walter Bau					
Ref.Ind.: CDAX	7.22%	7.61%	7.74%	5.95%	-2.84%
Ref.Ind.: Con. World	5.44%	6.66%	7.94%	6.00%	-2.81%
CAR values of DYWIDAG					
Ref.Ind.: CDAX	-7.12%	-0.94%	-3.22%	-1.60%	-0.97%
Ref.Ind.: Con. World	-9.11%	-2.09%	-3.21%	-1.61%	-1.00%
CAR values of Walter Bau & DYWIDAG combined					
Ref.Ind.: CDAX	2.36%	4.64%	4.16%	3.54%	-2.21%
Ref.Ind.: Con. World	0.51%	3.63%	4.29%	3.57%	-2.20%

Table 4.7 illustrates the CAR of Walter Bau, DYWIDAG and the combined entity at the acquisition announcement of the German DYWIDAG. In the results in the upper rows of each observation entity, I apply the German leading index CDAX as the reference index. In the results in the lower rows, I apply the World Construction index as the reference index.

The acquirer Walter Bau gained significant CAR of more than 7% on most event windows. DYWIDAG suffered strong losses from the acquisition. Considering the almost similar assumed corporate values of DYWIDAG and Walter Bau, the yields for Walter Bau on the 41-day event window mainly resulted from the losses at DYWIDAG. Overall, the acquisition created shareholder wealth in the short run, as the wealth effects illustrate for the combined entity. Corresponding to the Heilit Wörner acquisition, wealth was transferred from the target to the acquirer, but in total the discounts at DYWIDAG were more than offset by the gains of the Walter Bau shareholders. With the DYWIDAG acquisition, the findings of Denis et al. (2002) as well as Mentz and Schiereck (2008) that business-related domestic acquisitions benefit the acquirer also seemed overall to apply in the short-term perspective. The picture changes drastically when the observation time horizon is extended to six months or more.

In the long run, the positive impacts from the wealth transfer from the profitable target to the unprofitable acquirer vanished. In contrast, Walter Bau deteriorated a significant portion of its market value. While the acquisition of Heilit Wörner only led to underperformance of -20% to their domestic competitors in the 12-months observation horizon, the acquisition of the DYWIDAG performance difference even raised to -60% after 12 months and to -155% after 36 months. This divergence of share performance, particularly the value above 100%, implies a performance increase of the competitors, and on the other hand, a performance fall of Walter Bau after the acquisition. Indeed, the revenues declined by 24% in the following years. The financial results after the acquisition did not become positive as announced by the Walter Bau management (Börsen-Zeitung, 2001b) but dropped to a net loss of € -60mn within six months and to € -253mn after 12 months. The domestic construction building segment, the core business of both merged parties, with a loss of € -94mn, was responsible for this slump. Additionally, the merger caused a negative impact on the financial results of € -41mn due to restructuring and compensation expenses for the discharge of 1,600 employees (Walter Bau, 2002; Süddeutsche Zeitung, 2001). In the following years, neither the expected merger synergies of € 130mn annually nor a turnaround to a positive profitability was accomplished. The core business of the merged company, the domestic building construction unit, contributed exclusively losses. Only the internationally oriented DSI unit consistently reported positive profits to the headquarters (Walter Bau, 2002–2004).

Table 4.8: Acquisition of DYWIDAG – BHAR Values

Event Window	**36 Months**	**24 Months**	**12 Months**	**6 Months**	**3 Months**
BHAR of Walter Bau to Indices					
Ref.Ind.: CDAX	-33.62%	-26.38%	-44.82%	-10.74%	7.77%
Ref.Ind.: Con. World	-79.66%	-61.67%	-59.87%	-24.17%	0.55%
BHAR of Walter Bau to Reference Firms					
Mean	-154.98%	-80.60%	-62.48%	-13.14%	1.05%
Median	-156.22%	-94.88%	-61.33%	-8.56%	7.48%

Table 4.8 illustrates the BHAR values of Walter Bau after the acquisition of DYWIDAG. At the results in the first two rows, I compare the buy and hold returns of Walter Bau with those of the German leading index CDAX and the World Construction index. In the third and fourth rows, I compare the buy and hold returns of Walter Bau with big German competitors.

In spite of these overall difficulties from most operating units as well as the high expenses for the integration of DYWIDAG, Walter Bau documented slight positive results in 2002 and 2003. However, these earnings were not achieved by profitable operations but by the divestiture of several DYWIDAG premises (Walter Bau, 2003 and 2004). The concern Walter Bau would use the acquisition to rehabilitate its tense profitability situation seemed partly to be reasonable.

Concluding, neither the intention to benefit from the more profitable domestic targets nor Walter Bau's strategy to gain significant market power on the declining German market paid off for Walter Bau. Despite these acquisitions, the German construction market remained too fragmented to achieve higher returns from a market dominating position. In contrast, the domestic acquisitions increased the financial crisis of Walter Bau. After the takeover of DYWIDAG, the revenues and profitability dropped, and the equity-to-assets ratio declined to 10% as the net losses reduced the equity capital and further bank credits were required to finance the acquisition. That tenuous situation caused first rumors of a probable insolvency in 2002 (Geiger, 2002). Shortly before the insolvency, Walter Bau tried to purchase the solvent Züblin AG in order to avoid the impending liquidation.

4.4.4 The Acquisition Attempt of Züblin

In 2002 and 2003, Walter Bau intended to sell its 48.7% stake in the Züblin AG to the second big blockholder of Züblin, the Lenz family. The Lenz family owned a 42.7% stake in Züblin. Nevertheless, the Lenz family was reluctant to pay the € 180mn book value of Züblin to Walter Bau. Instead they decided to sell their stake to Walter Bau in 2004. On October 18, 2004, Walter Bau announced that it would acquire Züblin, the fifth-largest German construction firm. The capital market reacted to the acquisition announcement with abnormal returns of up to 6.76% for the Walter Bau share.

Table 4.9: Acquisition Attempt of Züblin – CAR Values

Event Window	[-20,+5]	[-10,+5]	[-5,+5]	[-3,3]	[-1,+1]
CAR values of Walter Bau					
Ref.Ind.: CDAX	4.87%	2.09%	6.76%	4.85%	0.13%
Ref.Ind.: Con. World	3.44%	1.79%	6.14%	4.81%	0.22%

Table 4.9 illustrates the CAR values of Walter Bau at the acquisition announcement of Züblin. In the results in the upper row, I apply the German leading index CDAX as the reference index. In the results in the lower row, I apply the World Construction index as the reference index. Since there are only a couple of weeks between the acquisition announcement and its rejection, the observation period after the announcement is reduced to a maximum of one week to avoid overlapping event windows.

The results indicate that the capital market assumed strong benefits for Walter Bau from the integration of Züblin. When comparing the economic development of both firms during the years before the acquisition attempt, the benefits can easily be explained. As aforementioned, Walter Bau documented revenue declines of more than 23% since 2000 and suffered from unprofitable operations. Contrarily, Züblin operated profitably and maintained the revenues on the same level during the years of the German construction recession. Furthermore, Züblin generated constant positive cash flows and reported more advantageous cash ratios than Walter Bau. Walter Bau's cash ratio dropped by ca. 44% from a value of 0.53 in 2000 to 0.30 in 2003, harming the solvency of the company (Walter Bau, 2001 and 2004). Walter Bau blamed the worse payment behavior of customers, especially of public authorities, for this development (Frankfurter Allgemeine Zeitung, 2004). This accusation partly applied to the decreasing liquidity, as the percentage of receivables on current assets increased by 71% and on total assets by 38% within the four years. Nonetheless, the two previous acquisitions also caused high extraordinary expenses for the integration of the targets. These takeovers required further bank loans for Walter Bau, which also raised the interest rate burdens and diminished the company's liquid funds (Walter Bau, 2002–2004).

Regardless of the reasons for this dilemma, the liquidity continued to decline drastically by -43% in the first six months of 2004. At the end of June, only € 126mn remained as liquid funds for Walter Bau (Frankfurter Allgemeine Zeitung, 2004). With the acquisition of Züblin, Walter Bau would have received the access of € 180mn liquid funds and avoided struggling for new bank loans. Hence, the acquisition would have supported Walter Bau in obtaining the desperately required liquidity (Financial Times, 2004). Nonetheless, the acquisition did not occur due to the resistance of the Federal Bank of Baden-Württemberg (Handelsblatt, 2005). The capital market penalized the decision with harsh abnormal losses for the Walter Bau share as the subsequent CAR analysis depicts.

Table 4.10: Rejection of Züblin Acquisition – CAR Values

Event Window	[-5,+20]	[-5,+10]	[-5;+5]	[-3,3]	[-1,+1]
CAR values of Walter Bau					
Ref.Ind.: CDAX	-22.08%	-23.99%	-13.87%	-15.98%	-18.55%
Ref.Ind.: Con. World	-23.87%	-25.00%	-12.79%	-15.61%	-18.52%

Table 4.10 illustrates the CAR values of Walter Bau at the acquisition rejection of Züblin through the Federal Bank of Baden-Württemberg. In the results in the upper row, I apply the German leading index CDAX as the reference index. In the results in the lower row, I apply the World Construction index as the reference index. Since there are only a couple of weeks between the acquisition announcement and its rejection, the observation period before the rejection is reduced to a maximum of one week to avoid overlapping event windows.

Due to this rejection, Walter Bau again faced strong challenges to find new liquid funds. In addition, the rejection and the subsequent strong abnormal losses of partly more than -20% supported the declining confidence of the market in the business of Walter Bau. Consequently, contractors assumed extensive disavowals at Walter Bau and retained advance payments. As initially mentioned, banks also refrained from a sustainability of Walter Bau and rejected further guaranteed bank credits, sealing the insolvency of Walter Bau. Deferring from this development, it seems as if the acquisition attempt of Züblin was purposed to secure the liquidity of Walter Bau, instead of strengthening the market power. Hence, it remains vague whether the positive abnormal returns at the acquisition announcement can serve as a strengthening argument for the benefit of domestic takeovers for bidding companies.

Although the free-float of the shares only accounted for 19% of the total capital, the capital market showed clear short-term reactions to all of Walter Bau's acquisitions announcements. The first reactions also highly correspond to the overall findings in the M&A research: Domestic acquisitions are superior to international diversification. However, there are three remarkable particularities at the short-term capital market reactions. The domestic targets Heilit Wörner and DYWIDAG, remarkably lost on the M&A transaction announcement, implying a wealth transfer from the targets to the acquirer and also negative effects of the M&A announcements for at least one involved party. Second, the longer the event window became, the lower the abnormal returns for Walter Bau became. When analyzing the long-term performance to comparable German construction firms, Walter Bau even extremely underperformed, indicating costly difficulties instead of positive synergies from the acquisitions. Third, Walter Bau suffered ca. five times as high losses after the rejection of the Züblin transaction, as they yielded abnormal returns at the prior acquisitions announcement of Züblin. It seems as if the capital market expected strong difficulties for Walter Bau if not acquiring Züblin. Since Züblin had plenty of liquid funds and Walter Bau was close to insolvency and several banks were reluctant to provide further credits to Walter Bau at the takeover attempt, the capital market analysts might have seen the acquisition as a remedy for Walter Bau to obtain access to liquid funds. This supports the assumption that the financially stricken Walter Bau would have used the takeover of Züblin for its own rehabilitation purposes. Apart from this hypothetical positive effect from the integration of Züblin, Walter Bau increased its financial burdens with all acquisitions. However, the intensity of the financial struggles after the domestic acquisitions are by far higher than after the international acquisition and even might also have had an impact on the insolvency of Walter Bau.

4.5 Conclusion

Most studies state a positive wealth effect for acquirers from domestic acquisitions of competitors as well as a superiority of domestic to international acquisitions (Denis et al., 2002; Mentz and Schiereck, 2008). In our study, however, I show that in certain circumstances, as highly fragmented markets combined with declining market volumes, this assumption must be reconsidered in particular for the long-term observation. Since the German construction market consistently underwent declining market volumes from 1995–2004, I analyze the wealth effects of the third biggest German construction firm Walter Bau, which mainly concentrated its business, including its M&A activities, on the home market. The observed acquisitions include a foreign takeover to compare the domestic with the foreign acquisitions. I illustrate by the means of a short-term event study, a long-term buy-and-hold abnormal return analysis as well as a performance analysis of accounting data that all acquisitions had value destructive effects, even though the short-term CAR values indicate ambiguous wealth impacts. The announcement of the foreign acquisition in 1995 caused first positive, but afterwards negative effects for Walter Bau. Hence, the capital market reversed its first positive into negative expectations for Walter Bau from that acquisition. Although the negative expectations became fact in the following years, they did not result from the international diversification process itself, but from operative mistakes and past burdens of the Australian subsidiary.

From the domestic takeovers, Walter Bau shortly gained abnormal returns. In contrast, the targets heavily lost on the acquisition announcement, implying a wealth transfer from the targets to Walter Bau, which supports the assumption that Walter Bau used the takeovers to camouflage its economic tense situation. For the combined entity, the domestic takeovers appeared slightly advantageous in the short run. However, at longer event periods, these benefits continuously decreased and reversed even negatively in the acquisition of Heilit Wörner, denoting the diminishing confidence of the market into these acquisitions.

In the long run, this tendency becomes more distinct and stresses the inferiority of the domestic transactions to the international acquisition. At the foreign takeover, the BHAR underperformance amounted in its peak to -40% in comparison to the world construction index and to -20% to the benchmark competitors. At the domestic acquisitions, these negative BHAR values dropped to -80% and even -155% respectively. In the observed case, the extraordinary integration costs of the targets in combination with operational difficulties even led to the insolvency of the firm.

To conclude, the observed M&A strategy of Walter Bau increased the difficulties of the conglomerate. Particularly, the domestic acquisitions caused fundamental problems for the company and demonstrated stronger negative effects than the international acquisition. Hence, acquisitions in a declining market with declining profitability margins seem to intensify the difficulties for the acquirer instead of serving as a remedy.

5 Conclusion

This doctoral thesis illustrates the wealth effects of M&A transactions within the construction industry. Despite the general findings of negative impacts of M&A on the bidder wealth in cross-industrial studies (Loughran and Vijh, 1997; Rau and Vermaelen, 1998; Andrade et al., 2001; Moeller et al., 2005), I find a distinct picture for the construction industry due to the uniqueness of the products and its high fragmentation that causes low profit margins and a tense economic situation for the construction sector. Hence, my findings explain whether M&A serve as a remedy for construction firms to improve their economic situation or whether a M&A strategy is superior within the construction industry.

To accomplish these objectives, I discuss in three studies the crucial aspects of M&A within the construction industry and its impact on corporate wealth. The first study focuses on short-term wealth effects in respect to a M&A announcement. As assumed the positive wealth effects for the bidding companies show a distinct picture different of those from cross-industrial studies. Within the construction industry acquirers achieve abnormal returns from M&A. In line with Denis et al. (2002), Goergen and Renneboog (2004) as well as Mentz and Schiereck (2008) horizontal or vertical acquisitions with a domestic focus is the superior strategy for acquiring construction firms. Non-construction firms gain most from conglomerate takeovers of construction firms whereas the geographical focus is of secondary relevance. The investigation of the bidders' wealth effects from M&A in the construction industry is also the focus of the second survey. In this study, I concentrate on the impacts of an acquisition on the long-term corporate performance. Again, the overall results show a positive effect for bidders from acquisitions in the construction industry. The last study analyzes whether the general findings from the first two studies also apply to certain market circumstances. Therefore, I investigate by means of a case study of the M&A strategy of a construction firm in a market with declining construction volumes. Under such conditions the overall positively rewarded horizontal acquisitions in the domestic market convert into a crucial drawback for the bidding company, as market dominance cannot be achieved in a fragmented industry like the construction sector.

The overall findings of all three studies may be of major relevance for managers of construction firms and non-construction firms. The results from the first two studies suggest that M&A indeed serve as a remedy for construction firms to enhance their tense economic situation. Construction firms particularly gain from strengthening their core business by purchasing competitors or from an extension to construction related businesses. With a bigger firm size construction companies might be more successful at bidding for lucrative large-scale projects and to improve their profit margins. An extension to up- or downstream services such as facility management contributes stables revenue streams to the rather volatile construction project business. Nevertheless, the findings from the case study imply no remarkable impact for an increase in market power from horizontal acquisitions. The high fragmentation of the construction sector seems to prevent any remarkable concentration structures within the construction industry at the current stage. The benefits from geographical diversification are twofold for construction firms. In the short-term perspective the international acquisitions show disadvantageous wealth effects for construction firms, which however turn positive in the long run. Domestic acquisitions yield positive impacts for construction firms on the short- and long-run perspective and seem to be superior to the internationalization strategy when both observation periods are considered. Nonetheless, this superiority mainly results from acquisitions in countries with strong real estate cycles. Otherwise, domestic concentration cannot be accounted as superior to internationalization. In the case of countries with decreasing construction volumes it becomes even the inferior strategy for construction firms. Consequently, construction firms are requested to analyze profoundly the market situation in which the chosen target operates next to the due diligence of the target itself.

Non-construction firms also gain from M&A transactions within the construction industry regardless whether their business is related or unrelated to the construction sector. They especially yield these benefits by incorporating sensitive and valuable construction knowledge for their complex construction projects. For example, mining companies require specific and generally expensive construction services for their mining activities and plants. In addition, incorporating construction services within the company increases the flexibility of non-construction firms to initiate a new construction project. This becomes a particular valuable asset in times of economic boom, when construction capacities limits are reached and prices for construction services rise. Similarly, REITs and private equity funds accomplish remarkable abnormal returns when adding construction companies to their investment portfolio. This positive outcome mainly results from the transfer of crucial business knowledge from the investor to the construction firm as well as a successful restructuring of the construction firm towards higher profitability. In addition, non-construction companies understand to successfully scatter its business on a global scale. Not surprisingly, internationalization by cross-border takeovers seems to be the superior strategy for non-construction firms.

Finally, the thesis sheds further light into the M&A research. Since the construction industry possesses several peculiarities the investigation of M&A transactions and corporate wealth leads to distinct results. My findings for M&A within the construction industry deviate from cross-industrial M&A surveys, but correspond to Gregory and McCorriston (2005), whose study implies different results from industry-specific surveys. Consequently, the three studies provide a promising prospect for further industry-specific M&A surveys.

Reference List

Actividades de Construccion y Servicios, 2004: Annual Report 2003, Madrid.

Aggarwal, Rajesh K./Samwick, Andrew A., 2003: Why Do Managers Diversify Their Firms? Agency Reconsidered, *Journal of Finance*, Vol. 58, No. 1, pp. 71-118.

Amihud, Yakov/Dodd, Peter/Weinstein, Mark, 1986: Conglomerate Mergers, Managerial Motives and Stockholder Wealth, *Journal of Banking and Finance*, Vol. 10, No. 2-3, pp. 401-410.

Anand, Jaideep, 2005: M&A Strategies in Mature and Declining Industries: Theoretical Perspectives and Implications, *Advances in Mergers and Acquisitions*, Vol. 4, pp. 163-179.

Andrade, Gregor/Mitchell, Mark/Stafford, Erik, 2001: New Evidence and Perspectives on Mergers, *Journal of Economic Perspectives*, Vol. 15, No. 2, pp. 103-120.

Angwin, Duncan, 2007: Motive Archetypes in Mergers and Acquisitions (M&A): The Implications of a Configurational Approach to Performance, *Advances in Mergers and Acquisitions*, Vol. 6, pp. 77-105.

Antoniou, Antonios/Petmezas, Dimitri/Zhao, Huainan, 2007: Bidder Gains and Losses of Firms Involved in Many Acquisitions, *Journal of Business Finance and Accounting*, Vol. 34, No. 7/8, pp. 1221-1244.

Asquith, Paul, 1983: Merger Bids, Market Uncertainty and Stockholder Returns, *Journal of Financial Economics*, Vol. 11, No. 2, pp. 51-83.

Austin, Christopher E., 1992: Drawing a Regulatory Road Map from the Hanson-Beazer Merger, *Mergers&Acquisitions*, Vol. 07/08 1992, p. 48.

Ball, Michael, 1996: Housing and Construction – A troubled Relationship, Bristol: Policy Press.

Barber, Brad M./Lyon, John D., 1997: Detecting Long-Run Abnormal Stock Returns: The Empirical Power and Specification of Test Statistics, *Journal of Financial Economics*, Vol. 43, No. 3, pp. 341-372.

Barlow, James/Jashapara, Ashok, 1998: Organisational Learning and Inter-Firm "Partnering" in the UK Construction Industry, *The Learning Organisation*, Vol. 5, No. 2, pp. 86-98.

Beach, Roger/Webster, Margaret/Campbell, Kerrie M., 2005: An Evaluation of Partnership Development in the Construction Industry, *International Journal of Project Management*, Vol. 23, No. 8, pp. 611-621.

Beitel, Patrick/Schiereck, Dirk/Wahrenburg, Mark, 2004: Explaining M&A Success in European Banks, *European Financial Management*, Vol. 10, No. 1, pp. 109-139.

Berger, Philip G./Ofek, Eli, 1995: Diversification's Effect on Firm Value, *Journal of Financial Economics*, Vol. 37, No. 1, pp. 39-65.

Berkovitch, Elazar/Narayan, Mandayam P., 1993: Motives for Takeovers: An Empirical Investigation, *Journal of Financial Quantitative Analysis*, Vol. 28, No. 3, pp. 347-362.

Bickel, Peter J./Götze, Friedrich/van Zwet, Willem R., 1997: Resampling fewer than n Observations: Gain, Losses, and Remedies for Losses, *Statistica Sinica*, Vol. 7, pp. 1-31.

Bilfinger-Berger, 2005: Annual Report 2004, Mannheim.

Bilfinger-Berger, 2009: Unternehmensgründungen, Fusionen und Akquisitionen im Überblick, *http://www.bilfingerberger.de/C1257130005050D5/vwContentByKey/W26P8LGD840MARSDE/$FILE/bilfinger_unternehmensgründungen_20080821_de.pdf*, call date: 06/11/2009.

Black, Carolynn/Akintoye, Akintola/Fitzgerald, Eamon, 2000: An Analysis of Success Factors and Benefits of Partnering in Construction, *International Journal of Project Management*, Vol. 18, No. 6, pp. 423-434.

Bloomberg (eds.), 2008: Stock Prices Walter Bau, call date: 06/17/2008.

Boehmer, Ekkehart/Masumeci, Jim/Poulsen, Annette B., 1991: Event-Study Methodology under Conditions of Event-Induced Variance, *Journal of Financial Economics*, Vol. 30, pp. 1081-1110.

Börsen-Zeitung (eds.), 1999: „Traumhochzeit" im Walter-Bau-Konzern, *Börsen-Zeitung*, No. 240, 12/11/1999, p. 10.

Börsen-Zeitung (eds.), 2000a: Walter Bau zieht nach Heilit auch DYWIDAG ganz an sich, *Börsen-Zeitung*, No. 236, 12/06/2000, p. 11.

Börsen-Zeitung (eds.), 2000b Heilit Wörner-Streubesitz will sich wehren – Schutzgemeinschaft plant Klage gegen Umtauschverhältnis bei Fusion mit Walter Bau-AG, *Börsen-Zeitung*, No. 105, 06/02/2000, p. 15.

Börsen-Zeitung (eds.), 2001a: Neuer Bauriese ist rund 2 Mrd. DM wert, *Börsen-Zeitung*, No. 73, 04/13/2001, p. 10.

Börsen-Zeitung (eds.), 2001b: Armutszeugnis für Walter Bau, *Börsen-Zeitung*, No. 186, 09/26/2001, p. 1.

Bradley, Michael/Desai, Anand/Kim, Han, 1988: Synergistic Gains from Corporate Acquisitions and Their Division between the Stockholders of Target and Acquiring Firms, *Journal of Financial Economics*, Vol. 21, No. 1, pp. 3-40.

Bresnen, Mike/Marshall, Nick, 2000: Partnering in Construction: A Critical Review of Issues, Problems and Dilemmas, *Construction Management and Economics*, Vol. 18, No. 2, pp. 229-237.

Briscoe, Geoffrey/Dainty, Andrew R.J./Millet, Sarah, 2001: Construction Supply Chain Partnerships: Skills, Knowledge and Attitudinal Requirements, *European Journal of Purchasing and Supply Management*, Vol. 7, No. 4, pp. 243-255.

Brown, Stephan/Warner, Jerold, 1985: Using Daily Stock Returns: The Case of Event Studies, *Journal of Financial Economics*, Vol. 14, No. 1, pp. 3-31.

Bruner, Robert F., 1988: The Use of Excess Cash and Debt Capacitiy as a Motive for Merger, *Journal of Financial and Quantitative Analysis*, Vol. 23, No. 2, pp. 199-217.

Bruner, Robert F., 2002: Does M&A pay? A Survey of Evidence for the Decision Maker, *Journal of Applied Finance*, Vol. 12, No. 1, pp. 48-68.

Bundesanzeiger Jahresabschlüsse, 2006: Walter Bau AG in Liquidation – Annual Report 2004, release date: 10/16/2006.

Bundesanzeiger Jahresabschlüsse, 2008: Walter Bau AG in Liquidation – Annual Report 03/2005 – 12/2005, release date: 10/14/2008.

Campa, José M./Hernando, Ignacio, 2004: M&As Performance in the European Financial Industry, *Journal of Banking and Finance*, Vol. 30, No. 3, pp. 3367-3392.

Campa, José M./Hernando, Ignacio, 2006: Shareholder Value Creation in European M&As, *European Financial Management*, Vol. 10, No. 1, pp. 47-81.

Carhart, Mark M., 1997: On Persistence in Mutual Fund Performance, *Journal of Finance*, Vol. 52, No. 1, pp. 57-82.

Case, Karl E./Glaeser, Edward L./Parker, Jonathan A., 2000: Real Estate and the Macroeconomy, *Brookings Papers on Economic Activity*, Vol. 2000, No. 2, pp. 119-162.

Choi, Jongsoo/Russel, Jeffrey S., 2004: Economic Gains around Mergers and Acquisitions in the Construction Industry of the United States of America, *Canadian Journal of Civil Engineering*, Vol. 31, No. 3, pp. 513-525.

Claessens, Stijn/Djankov, Simeon/Fan, Joseph P.H./Lang, Larry H.P., 2003: When does Corporate Diversification matter to Productivity and Performance, *Pacific-Basin Finance Journal*, Vol. 11, No. 3, pp. 365-392.

Collins, Jamie D./Hitt, Michael A., 2006: Leveraging Tacit Knowledge in Alliances: The Importance of Using Relational Capabilities to Build and Leverage Relational Capital, *Journal of Engineering and Technology Management*, Vol. 23, No. 3, pp. 147-167.

Conklin, David W., 2005: Cross-border mergers and acquisitions: A response to environmental transformation, *Journal of World Business*, Vol. 40, No. 1, pp. 29-40.

Cowan, Arnold R./Sergeant, Anne M.A., 2001: Interacting Biases, Non-Normal Return Distributions and the Performance of Tests for Long-Horizon Event Studies, *Journal of Banking an Finance*, Vol. 25, No. 4, pp. 741-765.

Construction Industry Federation (eds.), 2007: Overview of Industry, *<http://www.cif.ie/asp/-section.asp?s=15>*, call date: 02/16/2008.

Corhay, Albert/Rad, Alireza T., 2000: International Acquisition and Shareholder Wealth – Evidence from the Netherlands, *International Review of Financial Analysis*, Vol. 9, No. 2, pp. 163-174.

Danbolt, Jo, 2004: Target Company Cross-Border Effects in Acquisitions into the UK, *European Financial Management*, Vol. 10, No. 1, pp. 831-859.

De, Sankar/Fedenia, Mark/Triantis, Alexander J., 1996: Effects of Competition on Bidder Returns, *Journal of Corporate Finance*, Vol. 2, No. 3, pp. 261-282.

Delaney, Frank T./Wamuziri, Sam C., 2004: The Impact of Mergers and Acquisitions on Shareholder Wealth in the UK Construction Industry, *Engineering, Construction and Architectural Management*, Vol. 11, No. 1, pp. 65-73.

DeLong, Gayle, 2001: Stockholder Gains from Focusing versus Diversifying Bank Mergers, *Journal of Financial Economics*, Vol. 59, No. 3, pp. 221-251.

Denis, David J./Denis, Diane K./Yost, Kevin., 2002: Global Diversification, Industrial Diversification and Firm Value, *Journal of Finance*, Vol. 57, No. 5, pp. 1951-1979.

Deutsche Bank Research, 2008: Construction Outlook USA, *http://dbresearch.db.com*, call date: 08/07/2008.

Dodd, P., 1980: Merger proposals management discretion and stockholder, *Journal of Financial Economics*, Vol. 8, No. 2, pp. 105-137.

Dos Santos, Marcelo B./Errunza, Vihang B./Miller, Darius P., 2008: Does Corporate Diversification Destroy Value? Evidence from Cross-Border Mergers and Acquisitions, *Journal of Banking and Finance*, Vol. 32, No. 12, pp. 2716-2724.

DYWIDAG (eds.), 1997: Annual Report 1996, Munich.

DYWIDAG (eds.), 1998: Annual Report 1997, Munich.

DYWIDAG (eds.), 1999: Annual Report 1998, Munich.

DYWIDAG (eds.), 2000: Annual Report 1999, Munich.

DYWIDAG (eds.), 2001: Annual Report 2000, Munich.

DYWIDAG (eds.), 2009: Geschichte der DYWIDAG, www.dywidag.de, call date: 07/27/2009.

Eckbo, Espen B., 1982: Horizonal Mergers, Collusion, and Stockholder Wealth, *Journal of Financial Economics*, Vol. 11, No. 1-4, pp. 241-273.

Eckbo, Espen B./Thorburn, Karin, 2000: Gains to Bidder Firms Revisited: Domestic and Foreign Acquisitions in Canada, *Journal of Financial and Quantitative Analysis*, Vol. 35, No. 1, pp. 1-25.

Egan, John, 1998: Rethinking Construction, *Department of Environment, Transport and the Regions and HMSO*, London.

Engineering News Record (eds.), 2006: The Top 225 International Contractors – New Competitors enter the Market, New York, 2006.

Eun, Cheol S./ Kolodny, Richard /Scheraga, Carl, 1996: Cross-border acquisitions and shareholder wealth: Test of synergy and internalization hypotheses, *Journal of Banking and Finance*, Vol. 20, No. 9 pp. 1559-1582.

Euroconstruct (eds.), 2001: The 54th Euroconstruct Conference - Summary Report, Copenhagen, June/2001.

Euroconstruct (eds.), 2004: The 57th Euroconstruct Conference - Summary Report, Stockholm, June/2004.

Euroconstruct (eds.), 2006: The 62nd Euroconstruct Conference - Summary Report, Munich, December/2006.

Euroconstruct (eds.), 2007: The 63rd Euroconstruct Conference - Summary Report, Prague, June/2007.

Euroconstruct (eds.), 2008: Financial Crisis hits European Construction Sector, *ifo-institute*, Vol. 61, No. 13, pp. 27-32.

Fama, Eugne F./Fischer, Lawrence/Jensen, Michael C./Roll, Richard, 1969: The Adjustment of Stock Prices to New Information, *International Economic Review*, Vol. 10, No. 1, pp. 1-21.

Fama, Eugene F., 1992: Efficient Capital Markets II, *Journal of Finance*, Vol. 46, No. 5, pp. 1575-1617.

Fama, Eugene F./French, Kenneth R., 1993: Common Risk Factors in the Returns on Stocks and Bonds, *Journal of Finance*, Vol. 33, No.1, pp. 3-56.

Fama, Eugene F., 1998: Market Efficiency, Long-Term Returns, and Behavioural Finance, *Journal of Financial Economics*, Vol. 49, No. 1, pp. 283-306.

Fan, Joseph P.H./Goyal, Vidhan K., 2006: On the Patterns and Wealth Effects of Vertical Mergers, *Journal of Business*, Vol. 79, No. 2, pp. 877-902.

Financial Times Deutschland (eds.), 2004: Walter Bau stärkt Geschäft in Deutschland, *Financial Times Deutschland*, No. 205/2004, p. 10.

Financial Times Deutschland (eds.), 2005: Walter Bau droht Zerschlagung, *Financial Times Deutschland*, No. 23/2005, p. 1.

Frankfurter Allgemeine Zeitung (eds.), 1999: Walter Bau und Heilit planen einen schnellen Zusammenschluss, *Frankfurter Allgemeine Zeitung*, 12/16/1999, p. 22.

Frankfurter Allgemeine Zeitung (eds.), 2004: Walter Bau: Schlechte Zahlungsmoral des Staates, *Frankfurter Allgemeine Zeitung*, No. 203/2004, p. 14.

Franks, Julian R./Harris, Robert S., 1989: Shareholder Wealth Effects of Corporate Takeovers: The U.K. Experience 1955-1985, *Journal of Financial Economics*, Vol. 23, No. 2, pp. 225-249.

Fuller, Kathleen/Netter, Jeffrey/Stegemoller, Mike, 2002: What Do Returns to Acquiring Firms Tell Us? Evidence from Firms that Make Many Acquisitions, *Journal of Finance*, Vol. 57, No. 4, pp. 1763-1793.

Gaertner, Christian/Seidel, Hagen, 2005: „Die Holding bin ich“, *Die Welt*, No. 20, 01/20/2005, p. 16.

Geiger, Michaela, 2002: Bei Walter Bau schmilzt die Liquidität, *Die Welt*, Vol. 52, No. 92, 04/20/2002, p. 15.

Glawon, Patrizia, 2009: Interview with P. Glawon, Leading Project Manager at HOCHTIEF, Interview Date: 03/27/2009.

Goergen, Marc/Renneboog, Luc, 2004: Shareholder Wealth Effects of European Domestic and Cross-Border Takeover Bids, *European Financial Management*, Vol. 10, No. 1, pp. 9-45.

Gonzáles, Manuel/Arruñada, Benito/Fernández, Alberto, 1998: Regulation as a Cause of Firm Fragmentation: The Case of the Spanish Construction Industry, *International Review of Law and Economics*, Vol. 18, No. 4, pp. 433-450.

Gort, Michael 1969: An Economic Disturbance Theory of Mergers, *The Quarterly Journal of Economics*, Vol. 83, No. 4, pp. 624-642.

Gosh, Aloke/Lee, Chi-Wen., 2000: Abnormal Returns and Expected Managerial Performance of Target Firms, *Financial Management*, Vol. 29, pp. 40-52.

Green, Milford B./Cromley, Robert G., 1982: The Horizontal Merger: Its Motives and Spatial Employment Impacts, *Economic Geography*, Vol. 58, No. 4, pp. 358-370.

Gregory, Alan/McCorriston, Steve, 2005: Foreign Acquisitions by UK Limited Companies: Short- and Long-Run Performance, *Journal of Empirical Finance*, Vol. 12, No. 1, pp. 99-125.

Grossmann, Sanford/Hart, Oliver, 1980: Takeover Bids, the Free-Rider Problem, and the Theory of the Corporation, *Bell Journal of Economics*, Vol. 11, pp. 42-64.

Haksever, Mehmet/Demir, Ismail H./Giran, Omer, 2001: Assessing the Benefits of Long-Term Relationships between Contractors and Subcontractors in the UK, *International Journal of Construction Market*, Vol. 3, No. 1, pp. 2-15.

Handelsblatt (eds.), 2004: Walter Bau übernimmt Züblin, *Handelsblatt*, No. 204/2004, p. 15.

Handelsblatt (eds.), 2005a: Rettung für Walter Bau weiter völlig offen, *Handelsblatt,* No. 14/2005, p. 10.

Handelsblatt (eds.), 2005b: Weitere Walter Bau Töchter melden Insolvenz an, *Handelsblatt,* No. 26/2005, p. 12.

Hauptverband der Deutschen Bauindustrie (eds.), 2002: Wichtige Baudaten, *Die Deutsche Bauindustrie*, Vol. 9/2002, pp. 1-2.

Heilit Wörner (eds.), 2000: Annual Report 1999, Munich.

HOCHTIEF (eds.), 2005: Annual Report 2004, Essen.

HOCHTIEF (eds.), 2007: Annual Report 2006, Essen.

HOCHTIEF (eds.), 2009: Geschichte, *http://www.hochtief.de/hochtief/71.jhtml*, call date: 06/17/2009.

Houston, Joel/James, Christopher M./Ryngaert, Michael D., 2001: Where Do Mergers Gains Come From? Bank Mergers from the Perspective of Insiders and Outsiders, *Journal of Financial Economics*, Vol. 19, No. 2, pp. 195-209.

Jensen, Michael C./Ruback, Richard S., 1983: The Market for Corporate Control: The Scientific Evidence, *Journal of Financial Economics*, Vol. 11, No. 1-4, pp. 5-50.

Jensen, Michael C., 1986: Agency Cost of Free Cash-Flow, Corporate Finance, and Takeovers, *The American Economic Review*, Vol. 76, No. 2, pp. 323-329.

Jensen, Michael C./Murphey, Kevin J., 1990: Performance Pay and Top-Management Incentives, *Journal of Political Economy*, Vol. 98, No. 2, pp. 225-264.

Jovanovic, Boyan/Braguinsky, Serguey, 2004: Bidder Discounts and Target Premia in Takeovers, *The American Economic Review*, Vol. 94, No. 1, pp. 46-56.

Kamann, Dirk-Jan F./Snijders, Chris/Tazelaard, Frits/Wellinga, Derk T., 2006: The Ties that bind: Buyer-Supplier Relations in the Construction, *Journal of Purchasing and Suppty Management*, Vol. 12, No. 1, pp. 28-38.

Koehn, Rüdiger, 2001: Walter Bau bei Fusion schwächer bewertet, *Financial Times Deutschland (eds.)*, 04/12/2001, p. 3.

Koehn, Rüdiger/Bein, Hans-Willy, 2001: Walter Bau drohen Verluste, *Financial Times Deutschland (eds.)*, 04/11/2001, p. 11.

Kothari, S.P./Warner, Jerold B., 1997: Measuring Long-Horizon Security Price Performance, *Journal of Financial Economics*, Vol. 43, No. 3, pp. 301-339.

Lang, Larry H.P./Stulz, René M., 1994: Tobin's Q, Corporate Diversification, and Firm Performance, *Journal of Political Economy*, Vol. 102, No. 6, pp. 1248-1280.

Latham, Michael, 1994: Constructing the Team, HMSO, London.

Laussel, Didier., 2008: Buying Back Subcontractors: The Strategic Limits of Backward Integration, *Journal of Economics and Management Strategy*, Vol. 17, No. 4, pp. 895-911.

Levin, Dan/Peck, James, 2003: To Grab for the Market or to Bide One's Time: A Dynamic Model of Entry, *Rand Journal of Economics*, Vol. 34, No. 3, pp. 536-566.

Lewellen, Wilbur G., 1971: A Pure Financial Rationale for the Conglomerate Merger, *Journal of Finance*, Vol. 26, No. 2, pp. 521-537.

Li, Heng/Cheng, Eddie W.L./Love, Peter E.D./Irani, Zahir, 2001: Cooperative Benchmarking: A Tool for Partnering Excellence in Construction, *International Journal of Project Management*, Vol. 19, No. 3, pp. 171-179.

Lins, Karl/Servaes, Henri, 1999: International Evidence on the Value of Corporate Diversification, *Journal of Finance*, Vol. 54, No. 6, pp. 2215-2239.

Loughran, Tim/Vijh, Anand M., 1997: Do Long-Term Shareholders benefit from Corporate Acquisitions?, *Journal of Finance*, Vol. 52, No. 5, pp. 1765-1790.

Loughran, Tim/Ritter, Jay R., 2000: Uniformly Least Powerful Tests of Market Efficiency, *Journal of Financial Economics*, Vol. 55, No. 3, pp. 361-389.

Lu, Shaokai/Yan, Hong, 2007: An Empirical Study of Incentives of Strategic Partnering in China: Views from Construction Companies, *International Journal of Project Management*, Vol. 25, No. 3, pp. 241-249.

Lyon, John D./Barber, Brad M./Tsai, Chih-Ling, 1999: Improved Methods for Tests for Long-Run abnormal Stock Returns, *Journal of Finance*, Vol. 54, No. 1, pp. 165-201.

MacKinlay, Craig A., 1997: Event Studies in Economics and Finance, *Journal of Economic Literature*, Vol. 35, No. 1, pp. 13-39.

Manager Magazin (eds.), 2001: Walter Bau: Die eigenwilligen Methoden von Ignaz Walter sein Imperium zu retten, *Manager Magazin*, No. 6/2001, pp. 20-22.

Manager Magazin (eds.), 2005: Unter Wasser, *Manager Magazin*, No. 2/2005, pp. 46-50.

Markides, Constantinos C./Ittner, Christopher D., 1994: Shareholder Benefits from Coporate International Diversification: Evidence from U.S. International Acquisitons, *Journal of International Business Studies*, Vol. 25, No. 4, pp. 343-366.

Martin, John D./Sayrak, Akin, 2003: Corporate Diversification and Shareholder Value: A Survey of recent Literature, *Journal of Corporate Finance*, Vol. 9, No. 1, pp. 37-57.

McGraw-Hill Construction (eds.), 2006: Key Trends in the Construction Industry 2006 –Smart Market Report, New York.

McGraw-Hill Construction (eds.), 2007: Key Trends in the Construction Industry 2007 –Smart Market Report, New York.

McInish, Thomas H./Wood, Robert A., 1986: Adjusting for Beta Bias: An Assessment of Alternative Techniques: A Note, *Journal of Finance*, Vol. 41, No. 1, pp. 277-286.

Mentz, Markus/Schiereck, Dirk, 2008: Cross-Border Mergers and the Cross-Border Effect: The Case of the Automotive Supply Industry, *Review of Managerial Science*, Vol. 2 , pp. 199-218.

Ministry of Land, Infrastructure and Transport of Japan (eds.), 2008: Summary of Economic Construction Statistics, Tokyo.

Miozzo, Marcela/Dewick, Paul, 2002: Building competitive Advantage: Innovation and Corporate Governance in European Construction, *Research Policy*, Vol. 31, No. 6, pp. 989-1008.

Mitchell, Mark L./Stafford, Erik, 2000: Managerial Decisions and Long-Term Stock Price Performance, *Journal of Business*, Vol. 73, No. 3, pp. 287-329.

Moeller, Sara B./Schlingemann, Frederik P./Stulz, René M., 2004: Firm Size and the Gains from Acquisitions?, *Journal of Financial Management*, Vol. 73, No.2, pp. 201-228.

Moeller, Sara B./Schlingemann, Frederik P., 2005: Global Diversification and Bidder Gains: A Comparison between Cross-border and Domestic Acquisitions, *Journal of Banking and Finance*, Vol. 29, No. 3, pp. 533-564.

Moeller, Sara B./Schlingemann, Frederik P./Stulz, René M., 2005: Wealth Destruction on a massive Scale? – A Study of Acquiring-Firm Returns in the Recent Merger Wave, *Journal of Finance*, Vol. 60, No. 2, pp. 757-782.

Morck, Randall/Shleifer, Andrei/Vishny, Robert W., 1990: Do Managerial Objectives drive bad Acquisitions, *Journal of Finance*, Vol. 45, No. 1, pp. 31-48.

Morck, Randall/Yeung, Bernard, 1991: Why Investors value Multinationality, *Journal of Business*, Vol. 64, No. 2, pp. 165-187.

Morrow, J.L./Sirmon, David G./Hitt, Michael A./Holcomb, Tim R., 2007: Creating Value in the Face of Declining Performance: Firm Strategies and Organization Recovery, *Strategic Management Journal*, Vol. 28, pp. 271-283.

Nadolska, Anna/Barkema, Harry G., 2007: Learning to Internationalize: The Pace and Success of foreign Acquisitions, *Journal of International Business Studies*, Vol. 38, pp. 1170-1186.

National Bureau of Statistics China (eds.), 2006: China Statistical Yearbook 2005, Beijing.

National Bureau of Statistics China (eds.), 2008: China Statistical Yearbook 2007, Beijing.

New, Steve/Ramsey, John, 1997: A Critical Appraisal of Aspects of the Lean Chain Approach, *European Journal of Purchasing and Supply Management*, Vol. 3, No. 2, pp. 93-102.

Nocke, Volker/Yeaple, Stephen, 2007: Cross-Border Merger and Acquisitions vs. Greenfield Foreign Direct Investment: The Role of Firm Heterogeneity, *Journal of International Economics*, Vol. 72, pp. 336-365.

Officer, Micah S., 2007: The Price of Corporate Liquidity: Acquisition Discounts for Unlisted Targets, *Journal of Financial Economics*, Vol. 83, No. 4, pp. 571-598.

Pauser, Stephan/Rottke, Nico/Schiereck, Dirk, 2007: M&A in the Construction Industry – Wealth Effects of Diversification into Real Estate Life Cycle Related Services, *Working Paper #07-004, Real Estate Management Institute.*

Pesendorfer, Martin, 2003: Horizontal Mergers in the Paper Industry, *The Rand Journal of Economics*, Vol. 34, No. 3, pp. 495-515.

Petmezas, Dimitris, 2009: What drives Acquisitions? Market Valuations and Bidder Performance, *Journal of Multinational Financial Management*, Vol. 19, No. 1, pp. 54-74.

Phua, Florence T.T., 2006: When is Construction Partnering Likely to Happen? An Empirical Examination of the Role of Institutional Norms, *Construction Management and Economics*, Vol. 24, No. 6, pp. 615-624.

Rau, P. Raghavendra/Vermaelen, Theo, 1998: Glamour, Value and the Post-Acquisition Performance of Acquiring Firms, *Journal of Financial Economics*, Vol. 49, No. 2, pp. 223-253.

Research Institute of Construction and Economy (eds.), 2008: Summary 14th Asiaconstruct Conference, Tokyo, 10/2008.

Rice, Hugh L., 2007: Trends & Emerging Issues in the Construction Industry, *http://www.irmi.com/Confeences/Crc/Handouts/Crc257Tuesday/TrendsAndEmergingIssuesInTheConstructionIndustry.pdf*, call date: 03/12/2007.

Roll, Richard, 1986: The Hubris Hypothesis of Corporate Takeovers, *Journal of Business*, Vol. 59, No. 2, pp. 197-216.

Rottke, Nico/Wernecke, Martin, 2002: Management in Immobilienzyklen, *Immobilien Zeitung*, Vol. 1, pp. 1-49.

Rottke, Nico/Schiereck, Dirk/Vogt, Joachim, 2009: Consolidation, Value Chain Extension and Outside Industry Investors – Value Generating M&A Strategies in the Construction Industry, *SFA Conference Paper 2009*, http://www.etnpconferences.net/-sfa/sfa2009/User/Program.php.

Scholes, Myron /Williams, Joseph, 1977: Estimating Betas from Nonsynchronous Data, *Journal of Financial Economics*, Vol. 5, pp. 309-327.

Scott, Bob, 2001: Partnering in Europe – Incentive Based Alliancing for Projects, London: Thomas Telford Press.

Seidel, Hagen, 2004: Fusion von Walter Bau und Züblin steht auf der Kippe, *Die Welt*, Vol. 54, No. 284, 12/03/2004, p. 15.

Seth, Anju/Song, Kean/Pettit, Richardson, 2002: Value Creation and Destruction in Cross-Border Acquisitions: An Empirical Analysis of Foreign Acquisitions of U.S. Firms, *Strategic Management Journal*, Vol. 23, pp. 921-940.

Shao, Jun, 1996: Bootstrap Model Selection, *Journal of the American Statistical Association*, Vol. 91, No. 434, pp. 665-665.

Shleifer, Andrei/Vishny, Robert W., 1989: Management Entrenchment: The Case of Manager-Specific Investments, *Journal of Financial Economics*, Vol. 20, No. 1, pp. 123-139.

Singh, Harbir/Montgomery, Cynthia A., 1987: Corporate Acquisition Strategies and Economic Performance, *Strategic Management Journal*, Vol. 8, No. 4, pp. 337-386.

Singh, Manohar/Faircloth, Sheri, 2005: The Impacts of Corporate Debt on Long Term Investment and Firm Performance, *Applied Economics*, Vol. 5, No. 8, pp. 875-883.

Statistisches Bundesamt (eds.), 2008: Baugewerblicher Umsatz, www-genesis.destatis.de, call date: 10/15/2008.

Stein, Jeremy C., 1997: Internal Capital Markets and the Competition for Corporate Resources, *Journal of Finance*, Vol. 52, No. 1, p.111-133.

Stulz, René M./Walkling, Ralph A./Song, Moon H., 1990: The Distribution of Target Ownership and the Division of Gains in Successful Takeovers, *Journal of Finance*, Vol. 45, No. 3, pp. 817-833.

Sudarsanam, Puliyur/Mahate, Ashraf A., 2006: Are Friendly Acquisitions Too Bad for Shareholders and Managers? Long-Term Value Creation and Top-Management Turnover in Hostile and Friendly Acquirers, *British Journal of Management*, Vol. 17, pp. 7-30.

Süddeutsche Zeitung (eds.), 1997: Ergebniseinbruch bei Walter Bau – Für 1997 kaum Besserung erwartet/Dividende halbiert, *Süddeutsche Zeitung*, 05/21/1997, p. 19.

Süddeutsche Zeitung (eds.), 2001: Unternehmenswert rund zwei Milliarden DM – Walter Bau und DYWIDAG mit Verlust in die Fusion, *Süddeutsche Zeitung*, 04/14/2001, p. 25.

Süddeutsche Zeitung (eds.), 2004: SZ-Interview mit Ignaz Walter, Aufsichtratsvorsitzender der Walter Bau: „Wir sind kein Pleitefall", *Süddeutsche Zeitung*, 10/28/2004, p. 23.

Sutton, Clifton D., 1993: Computer-Intensive Methods for Tests about the Mean of an Asymmetrical Distribution, *Journal of the American Statistical Association*, Vol. 88, No. 423, pp. 802-808.

Swanstrom, Mark, 2006: Corporate Governance and the Abnormal Returns to Acquisition Announcements, *The Journal of Business Strategies*, Vol. 23, No. 2, pp. 115-129.

Thomson Financial (eds.), 2008: Deal and Corporate Analysis, call date: 01/10/2008.

Thomson Financial (eds.), 2009: Deal and Corporate Analysis, call date: 02/27/2009.

Travlos, Nickolaos G., 1987: Corporate Takeover Bids, Methods of Payment and Bidding Firms' Stock Returns, Journal of Finance, Vol. 42, No. 4, pp. 943-963.

Walter Bau (eds.), 1992: Annual Report 1991, Augsburg.

Walter Bau (eds.), 1993: Annual Report 1992, Augsburg.

Walter Bau (eds.), 1994: Annual Report 1993, Augsburg.

Walter Bau (eds.), 1995: Annual Report 1994, Augsburg.

Walter Bau (eds.), 1996: Annual Report 1995, Augsburg.

Walter Bau (eds.), 1997: Annual Report 1996, Augsburg.

Walter Bau (eds.), 1998: Annual Report 1997, Augsburg.

Walter Bau (eds.), 1999: Annual Report 1998, Augsburg.

Walter Bau (eds.), 2000: Annual Report 1999, Augsburg.

Walter Bau (eds.), 2001: Annual Report 2000, Augsburg.

Walter Bau (eds.), 2002: Annual Report 2001, Augsburg.

Walter Bau (eds.), 2003: Annual Report 2002, Augsburg.

Walter Bau (eds.), 2004: Annual Report 2003, Augsburg.

Walter Bau (eds.), 2005: Annual Report 2004, Augsburg.

Welling, Derk T./Kamann, Dirk-Jan F., 2001: Vertical Cooperation in the Construction Industry: Size Does Matter, Journal of Supply Chain Management, Vol. 37, No. 4, pp. 28-33.

Wernerfelt, Birger, 1984: A Resource Based View of the Firm, Strategic Management Journal, Vol. 5, No. 2, pp. 171-180.

White, Halbert, 1980: A Heteroskedasticity-Consistent Covariance Matrix and a Direct Test for Heteroskedasticity, Econometrica, Vol. 48, pp. 817-838.

Züblin (eds.), 2001: Annual Report 2000, Stuttgart.

Züblin (eds.), 2002: Annual Report 2001, Stuttgart.

Züblin (eds.), 2003: Annual Report 2002, Stuttgart.

Züblin (eds.), 2004: Annual Report 2003, Stuttgart.

Corporate Finance and Governance

Herausgegeben von Dirk Schiereck

Band 1 Sebastian Michael Gläsner: Return Patterns of German Open-End Real Estate Funds. An Empirical Explanation of Smooth Fund Returns. 2010.

Band 2 Patrick Ams: Directors' Dealings and Insider Trading in Germany. An Empirical Analysis. 2010.

Band 3 Joachim Vogt: Value Creation within the Construction Industry. A Study of Strategic Takeovers. 2011.

www.peterlang.de